Smarter and Healthier

Educational Information for Becoming a Fine Chef

by

Chef Patrick J. Gorey

DORRANCE
PUBLISHING CO
EST. 1920
PITTSBURGH, PENNSYLVANIA 15222

Dorrance Publishing Co., Inc.
701 Smithfield Street
Pittsburgh, PA 15222
Visit our website at *www.dorrancebookstore.com*

ISBN: 978-1-4809-0559-7
eISBN: 978-1-4809-0576-4

Acknowledgments

U.S. Food and Drug Administration

U.S. Department of Agriculture

Wikipedia, the free encyclopedia

A special thank-you to Aggie Sutton for her informative
contribution to the chapter "Gluten – Celiac Disease."

Table of Contents

To my wife, Carroll…

….for your love and invaluable assistance in preparing this book.

Author Profile

Chef Gorey was born and classically trained in Europe.

He began a National and Hotel industry-recognized, five-year practical European Culinary Apprenticeship training program in July 1954 at age 14 in the Metropole, a well-known, distinguished, popular and busy six-story entertainment and restaurant center with a French-themed departmental kitchen on the top floor, which serviced three separate restaurants, including a gourmet silver-service grill, and a ball-room-banquet room, located in the heart of Dublin. As part of the program, based on the fundamental principals of the renowned 19th century Master French Chef Auguste Escoffier (1846–1935), he studied as a "Commis Chef" (Assistant) for the first four years, and as an "Improver" or "Probationer" Chef (Stagiaire) for the fifth and final year.

He was slight of build, and needed a wooden box to stand on in order to reach the large commercial stoves when he first learned how to prepare Bechamel and other sauces. On his first day in the kitchen, he was posted to the vegetable department to peel potatoes, and chop and rinse fresh parsley.

Upon the successful completion of his apprenticeship, and because of reciprocity among European nations, he enhanced his culinary repertoire and craftsmanship by traveling and working away from home in order to gain additional experience, and as a result of the intense, quality training he received under Master chefs, he secured his first position as Chef de Cuisine, responsible for a brigade of Chefs, purchasing, writing menus, hiring and firing, and overall kitchen production at age twenty-one. He has since held various culinary positions such as Chef de Partie, Chef Tournant, Chef Garde Manger, Chef Patissier, Sous

Chef, Chef de Cuisine, and Executive Chef in 3-, 4-, and 5-star hotels, restaurants, and Country Clubs in Ireland, England, France, Channel Islands, and America.

He is proficient in hors d'oeuvre, soups, sauces, salads, seafood, entrees, vegetables, pastry and desserts, classic artistic buffets, gingerbread houses, pastilliage (sugar paste) buildings, ice carvings, wedding cakes, western European cuisine, and overall culinary artistry.

He has been an invited guest speaker at several institutions.

He has also been retained by International businessmen as their private Chef, sometimes on board private luxury yachts.

He is currently a freelance independent Culinary Consultant.

Introduction

This humble work is neither a medical, scientific, nor gastronomical encyclopedia, nor is it a complete manual or narrative on harmful bacteria. Unintentionally, I'm sure much is omitted. Over the years I have received numerous requests to write a cookbook, and after much consideration, I came to the sensible conclusion that there was a superabundance of recipe cookbooks published, so I decided against repeating what had already been successfully accomplished. Consequently, I have chosen to write about some of the world's more exquisite and costly food ingredients and bacteriological contamination, which may not be found in recipe cookbooks.

Speaking of recipes, this book contains only one single recipe...for Pate Brisee.

It is my adaptation from many different tests of varying ingredient amounts, and I am satisfied with this final composition and effort.

My primary purpose in writing this book is to impress upon young apprentice chefs, practicing chefs, and cooks of the indisputable importance of personal hygiene and sanitization in the kitchen, bathrooms, and elsewhere.

In preparing for this endeavor, I rummaged through a trove of my collection of handwritten notes, some of which I had saved from my very first days in the kitchen, and others, which as a practicing chef and culinary consultant I had collected from working with many slightly stooped, elderly, respected, gray-haired Master chefs of several nationalities throughout Europe, and then compiled them into this endeavor.

Those idols of mine were the generals of the kitchen, and one NEVER questioned their authority. Becoming a professional chef is a very, very long, arduous process. One needs to have the dream of becoming a chef in order to survive. The learning is unending. No single chef, no matter how worldly or famous, whether television, radio celebrity, or otherwise, does not and will never know everything. Every day, one learns something new, so take heart all you young apprentice chefs, novice cooks, and housewives, because chefs just like you are educating themselves on a daily basis.

It requires significant commitment of time and energy to master this craft, this chemistry, this culture, this art form. You cannot be egotistical, you have to like to be challenged, and I am empathetic towards anyone involved in the foodservice industry because I understand and appreciate how hard he or she labors.

In Europe in those early days, it was generally accepted knowledge that any apprentice who wanted to attain credibility must study and work in France. French cuisine without doubt embodies great history, excellence, and a needed pedigree for one's resume. France, and French chefs such as the Master, Auguste Escoffier, set the standard for exquisite cuisine on the world stage.

A professional kitchen is no place whatsoever for laziness. There is always a symphony of activity going on, and I would always teach my staff that they should consider the scheduled time for lunch and dinner to be synonymous with producing a Broadway show by telling them, "When the curtain goes up, we must all be ready to perform."

To become an "Executive Chef" one must have an impeccable resume, be born with a good, delicate palate, have a sensitive nose, be conscientious, possess an imaginative ability with experience in food flavors and aromas, be courageous and willing to explore new techniques and ingredients with new menu ideas, be able to handle criticism constructively, be extremely selective in hiring practices, respect staff, be sincere, be focused, and have a desire to train and educate young men and women toward a future in the culinary arts, and be able to maintain physical stamina in order to successfully complete those long, hot, rigorous ten-to-eighteen hour days, six days a week, catering to hundreds of guests daily.

The culinary world is an endlessly exciting craft with many positive and endearing points, such as respect from society, and meeting and making new friends either while traveling, vacationing, or simply taking a pleasant stroll in a park.

I have found that once someone discovers what you do, the conversation immediately turns to food, and before you know it, you are giving cooking tips and recipes while air-borne at 30,000 ft., or while swimming in a club pool. However, time, ego, relationships, social life, and humility, among others, are all sacrificed.

During my career, I have met and cooked for many wealthy, successful, and famous people. Unfortunately I have had one heartbreaking disappointment. In the autumn of 1968, I was approached by wealthy industrialist Edward L. Gruber with a request. He asked me to accompany him, and three other friends of his (the then-incumbent Pennsylvania Governor Raymond Shafer (1967–1971), the then-incumbent Pennsylvania State Senator Edwin G. Holl, and believe it or not, the former World War Two Allied Supreme Commander, and former U.S. President Dwight D. Eisenhower) on a one-week hunting and fishing trip to a private lodge deep in the Canadian wilderness. Two Secret Service agents and I were to round out the group. I was told that should I need to purchase any provisions, the nearest grocery store was one hundred miles by small private plane from the lodge.

My duties would include preparing early breakfast, lunch baskets, baking breads, and cooking whatever wild game and river and lake fish the guests would shoot or catch each day for dinner.

This for me was a "no-brainer" and I was ecstatic with excitement!

The first question I asked was not how much I would be paid, but, "Can I bring my camera?" All I thought about was the opportunity to take candid photos of Mr. Eisenhower, whom I admired. I was in the process of obtaining Secret Service security clearance when the bad news reached me…Mr. Eisenhower, who had retired close by to his farm in Gettysburg, Pennsylvania, had taken ill (He would later die on March 28, 1969 of congestive heart failure).

Naturally, the trip was cancelled. I was saddened beyond belief, and I still consider it the most regrettable incident of my entire culinary career.

I am a traditionalist and passionate about my craft. I believe chefs and apprentices should wear, as they have since the concept was first adopted in 1820, a white toque, white chef's jacket, white apron, and checkered hounds-tooth pants.

(The toque was a white version of the black hats of Greek Orthodox priests).

I am not appreciative of those ignorant and untrained so-called chefs who wear baseball caps, black or denim jackets, and wild, outrageous colorful pants. They are undignified, and they demean our profession.

This book contains my personal photographs, descriptions, and experiences, but not all of the text is the sole work of the author alone—I must give credit to all those exceptional genius chefs of long, long ago who taught and inspired me in the early years. I want this book to be a voice for cleanliness and sanitization in the foodservice industry, and perhaps the hints and ideas throughout this little volume will give you something to aim for. I would have greatly appreciated having it available to me when I first began my culinary journey over fifty years ago. I now pass it along to you with my very good wishes.

Patrick J. Gorey. (Chef) - 2013

Helpful Culinary Information, Hints, & Myths

The two most prestigious and influential culinary schools in the world are:

> Le Cordon Bleu
> 8 Rue Leon
> Delhomme, 75015
> Paris, France.
> Telephone: 33 (0) 1 53 68 22 50
> www.cordonbleu.edu

Le Cordon Bleu was founded in Paris, France, in 1895 by Marthe Distel.

AND

> The Culinary Institute of America
> 1946 Campus Drive
> Hyde Park, NY, U.S.A. 12538
> Telephone: (845) 452 9600
> www.ciachef.edu

The Culinary Institute of America was founded in Connecticut, U.S.A., in 1946 by Frances Roth and Katherine Angell as the "New Haven (CT) Restaurant Institute."

• • • • • • • • • •

- The highest award a restaurant can earn is the "Guide Michelin" three (3) star designation.
- The "Zagat Survey" is an excellent source of review of the world's restaurants, from the most elegant, to casual, inexpensive bistro's. Simply go to: Zagat.com
- Whenever possible, invoke the "Glove Rule" in the kitchen use either "Powder-Free Latex," or "High-Density Polyethylene." Polyethylene is preferable as some people suffer allergic reactions, symptoms, or discomfort, such as: hives, itching, breathing difficulties, or dizziness from the use of natural rubber latex. Single use of these gloves is imperative.
- It is essential to provide an alcohol- based hand -sanitizer dispenser in bathrooms, kitchens, and elsewhere where needed throughout the house or establishment.
- When carving ANY cooked meat, slice across the fibers, or grain, of the meat, NEVER along them. To do so is absolutely incorrect, and results in slices of tough, chewy, indigestible meat.
- Culinary mediocrity is unacceptable. In preparing food, it is imperative that it must firstly appeal to the eye, and (of course) secondly, that it is pleasing to the palate. Remember the old adages: "If you are not proud of it, don't serve it," and "When in doubt, throw it out."
- During a pause while dining, place the knife and fork with the point of the knife and the tines of the fork facing upward and inward towards the center of the plate to form an "A" on the plate. This tells the server you are just pausing and are not finished eating. When finished eating, place the knife, (with the blade facing left) and the fork, with the tines facing upward, close together in the center of the plate. This tells the server you are finished eating. (All this presumes the server is educated to what you are doing. If not...forget it!)
- Using the term "Shrimp Scampi" is confusing. The word "Scampi" is the Italian plural of "Scampo," a culinary word for "Prawn" (also known as "Norway Lobster," "Dublin Bay Prawn," or "Langoustine"). The Italian word for "Shrimp'" is "Gambero" or "Gamberetto" (singular). Monkfish is also sometimes called "Scampi." The word "Scampi" is used loosely on menus in the U.S.A. to describe the method of preparation of a shrimp dish. Therefore, it is

incorrect to say "Shrimp Scampi," as it is akin to saying "Shrimp Prawn."

- To achieve a golden brown glaze on fresh salmon when sautéing, sprinkle a mixture of light brown sugar, salt, cornstarch, and a pinch of cinnamon over the flesh side of the salmon prior to sautéing it in a medium, pre-heated non-stick sauté pan for two to three minutes on each side (depending on the thickness of the salmon) and allow the salmon to rest for two minutes before serving.
- Chinook salmon is highest in oil content.
- Fish stock should only be cooked for 20 minutes; otherwise it becomes bitter.
- Never cover a dish containing fresh cream while cooking. Doing so produces steam, which becomes water, and dilutes the sauce.
- It is a myth that you should never wash mushrooms before cooking. We all know what mushrooms are grown in, and sometimes a brush or paper towel is not enough to properly clean them. Therefore, the type of cleaning depends on how dirty they are.
- Lobsters do not have vocal chords, therefore it is a myth that they scream when you boil them. The whine you may hear is from superheated vapors whistling from the joints in the shell.
- Fresh oysters, clams, scallops, and mussels must be kept refrigerated and alive until they are to be opened for serving. The flat side of the oysters must face upward, and it is common practice to sprinkle them with corn meal to feed them.
- Wrap fresh celery in aluminum foil when storing in the refrigerator; it will keep for weeks.
- Fresh celery strips will become crisp and delicious if placed in iced water for a minimum of ten minutes with one teaspoon of sugar per quart of water.
- To freshen asparagus, stand the stems in iced water.
- To keep cauliflower white, cook in half water/half milk and boil uncovered.
- Sliced bananas or avocados won't turn black when dipped in lemon juice.
- Chocolate will become flexible when mixed with a little oil.
- Studies have shown that it is a myth that chocolate raises LDL (bad) cholesterol. Its saturated fat content is derived from Stearic acid, which does not perform like the common saturated fat. In fact, chocolate may lower cholesterol levels for some people.

Other studies suggest that some persons with diabetes may enjoy dark chocolate because of its ability to improve Endothelial Dysfunction. However, it is still wise to exercise caution by seeking medical advice from your doctor before partaking of a delicious 70 per cent Cacao chocolate bar known as "Food for the Gods," and which Casanova considered an aphrodisiac.

- Burned surfaces on food can be scraped off easily with a fine lemon grater.
- It is a myth that eating turkey makes you sleepy.
- "All Natural" chicken is not "Organic."
- "Chilled-Air," free-range organic chicken, as opposed to "Salt-Water Bath" chicken, is best because there is no salt absorption.
- When seasoning red meat or fish with salt, do it just before cooking, as the salt will draw out the natural juices prematurely.
- Never serve cucumbers with the skin on. Always peel them, and always slice them thinly.
- When serving red onions on a salad, slice them very thinly.
- To remove skin from tomatoes, make an "X" with a knife on each end and drop them in boiling water for 10 seconds, remove, and immediately drop them into iced water, then peel.
- Always remove the stem and eye areas from tomatoes before slicing and serving.
- Never re-freeze previously frozen thawed foods.
- To re-freshen stale dinner rolls, sprinkle them with water and place them in a hot oven for a few minutes.
- Store unused coffee granules in a tightly covered container in the freezer.
- To keep potatoes from budding, place an apple in a brown bag with them.
- When making mashed potatoes, NEVER add COLD milk or cream, as it will make them "starchy." Always scald the milk or cream before adding.
- If you accidentally over-salt a dish while it's still cooking, drop in a peeled potato. It absorbs most of the excess salt.
- Place a slice of apple or a slice of bread in hardened brown sugar to soften it back up.
- When boiling corn-on-the-cob, add a pinch of sugar and a small amount of milk to help bring out the corn's natural sweetness.

- Use a meat baster to "squeeze" pancake batter onto the hot griddle—perfectly shaped pancakes every time.
- Covering a hand held grater with wax paper will trap the zest of citrus fruit peel and save on the time it takes to clean up.
- Use a half-teaspoon of sugar when cooking all fresh vegetables to bring out flavor.
- Always triple wash fresh fruits and vegetables before use.
- Sour whipping cream may be turned to butter when beaten long enough.
- Glucose prevents sugar from crystallizing.
- Puff pastry should only be rolled on a marble slab that has been refrigerated or cooled with a tray of crushed ice set on top of it shortly before starting to roll the pastry.
- Add white vinegar to the water content for puff pastry and bake on a flat, wet sheet-pan for additional lifting power.
- Cherries will turn white when soaked in a vinegar-water solution.
- Bring vinegar to a boil in a new pan to prevent foods from sticking.
- Reduce cheap balsamic vinegar on the stove to enrich it.
- Aside from containing important vitamins and nutrients, apple cider vinegar is a powerful germ-killing acid when washing or cleaning counter-tops, cutting boards, and cooking utensils.
- Macaroons or cookies (biscuits) that stick to paper will come loose when set on a wet tabletop.
- A good orange should be firm and solid to the touch; lightweight oranges are dry and tasteless.
- Grapes will stay fresher longer in the refrigerator if left on the vine branch and not washed until ready for use.
- Alcohol does not cook out of every dish. Ethanol still remains, even if you cook it for hours.
- Frying slices of raw potato, a slice of bread, or a slice of lemon peel, in clouded hot fat will re-clarify and remove foreign flavors and sediment in the fat.
- To keep limes fresh, place them in a jar, cover, and store in the refrigerator.
- To slice very fresh bread easily, use a hot knife.
- It is a myth that parchment paper contains poisons. It can be heated to high temperatures without fear of contamination.
- Bacon will not curl if you dip it into ice-cold water, then tap it dry with a paper towel before frying.

- To prevent cheese from hardening, butter the outsides before storing, or wrap a cloth dampened with vinegar around the cheese.
- Thaw frozen fish in milk. The milk draws out the frozen taste and provides a fresh-caught flavor.
- Soak chicken in salted cold water for 10 minutes, then rinse in cold water and dry with a paper towel before cooking to remove blood and any possible bacteria.
- If a bag of sugar becomes lumpy, place it in the refrigerator for 24 hours.
- Cut a thin slice from each end of a potato in order to speed up the baking time.
- When peeling onions, you'll shed fewer tears if you: cut the root from the onion last, place the onions in the freezer for five minutes before peeling, or hold a slice of bread in your teeth while peeling onions.
- It is a myth that an unused, refrigerated cut onion becomes poisonous (unless it is then handled with dirty hands, or cut on a contaminated cutting board). A cut bulb onion contains enzymes that produce sulphuric acid, thereby eliminating the possibility of bacterial contamination.
- Ripen green fruits by placing them in a perforated plastic bag. The holes allow air movement, yet retain the odorless gas which fruits produce to promote ripening.
- When pan frying, always slightly heat the pan before adding butter or oil.
- A little salt sprinkled into the frying pan will prevent spattering.
- A few teaspoons of sugar and cinnamon slowly caramelized on top of the stove will hide unpleasant cooking odors.
- A tablespoon of olive oil added to water when boiling rice will prevent sticking. Do not use it when boiling pasta. Italian purists would cringe at the idea, as it prevents the sauce from clinging to the pasta.
- To get ketchup to flow out of the bottle evenly, insert a drinking straw, push it to the bottom of the bottle, and remove.
- Freeze leftover wine, chicken, beef or fish stock in ice cube trays for future use in sauces and casseroles.
- Rub raw potato slices over your hands and rinse to remove stains.
- Pre-salt the water for boiling potatoes, vegetables, and pasta, and season all foods early in the cooking process.

- Scientific research has discovered evidence that a component in garlic stimulates an enzyme that guards the stomach from the harmful effects of carcinogens, and it may lower the risk of heart disease, high blood pressure, and cholesterol.
- Eating excessive amounts of raw garlic can cause anemia. Cooked garlic is much easier on the digestive tract.
- Garlic contains protein, thiamine, riboflavin, niacin, and vitamin C.
- When chopping garlic cloves, put a tablespoon of water or a teaspoon of salt on the board with them to prevent splatter.
- Always "bloom" (soften) sheet gelatin in iced water in order to prevent it from losing any power.
- Don't mix light colored foods in an aluminum pot; this may turn them gray.
- Use a very fine balloon whisk for making a smooth, velvety-textured sauce.
- Goat cheeses are healthier than cow cheeses.
- Avoid eating salads in tropical locations.
- When you get a splinter, apply scotch adhesive tape over the splinter and remove.
- To cure a headache, cut a lime in half and rub it on your forehead.
- For itch from mosquito bites, apply soap to the area.
- To open fruit jars easily, set the jar upside down in hot water for a few minutes.
- To keep cutting boards or bowls from slipping on a counter-top, place them on a damp cloth.
- To remove burnt-on food from a pot or skillet, add a tablespoon of pure baking soda or dish soap with enough water to cover the bottom of the pan or pot, bring it to a boil and let it rest for 15 minutes, then clean.
- Pure baking soda (Sodium Bicarbonate) may be used as an antacid, and to remove soil, dirt, wax, and residue from fresh vegetables and lettuces by rinsing them in a bowl of cold water and the baking soda.
- To remove coffee, tea, or cigarette stains from fine china, rub with a damp cloth dipped in baking soda.
- Silver will gleam after a rubbing with damp baking soda on a soft cloth.

- Oxidation of metal in pots or bowls can be removed with salt and lemon juice.
- To remove lime deposit from a tea kettle, fill it with equal parts of vinegar and water, bring it to a boil, and allow it to stand overnight.

Bacteria & Food Handling Safety Procedures

A recent study revealed that only 33% of restaurant employees had received any training in cleanliness and food allergy safety. I am appalled by this statistic.

Nothing...and I mean...nothing, is more important than strict, proper, safe, and sanitary food preparation processes in order to safeguard against the risk of bacteriological contamination, viruses, pathogens, parasites, allergies, food-intolerances, and other food-borne illnesses, some of which may cause blindness, cancer, and death.

The U.S. Food and Drug Administration (FDA) estimates there are 75 million cases and 3,000 deaths in the U.S. annually from food-borne illnesses.

The technical term for bacteria is "Pathogenic Microorganism," and it is my sincere wish that "Smarter and Healthier" with its reasonable number of ideas, hints, anecdotes, quotations, pet-peeves, do-not's, historical data, definitions, tales, facts, and myths related to food will awaken an interest through its condensed scientific knowledge and information, and will lead the reader to deeper thought and a broader study of the necessary precautions culinarians (and all people!) should and must practice in order to avoid food-borne illnesses. This chapter will provide proprietors, managers, executive chefs, practicing chefs, apprentice chefs, novice cooks, maitre D's, waiters, waitresses, butlers, hosts, hostesses, and indeed all culinarians with an increased knowledge of the wonderful world of La Haute Cuisine, thereby safeguarding the unsuspecting customer or guest from contracting food poisoning, and in turn protect food service establishments from legal ramifications.

As a professional chef, and on a personal level, I am fastidious about culinary sanitation and bacteriological contamination. The study of food-borne illnesses is a subject that I pay special attention to, and which rightfully should demand the highest consideration from all. Therefore, I strongly urge everyone to give society, and yourselves, a tremendously inexpensive gift. Sanitize, sanitize, sanitize.

I do feel that the time is long past when instruction of the principals of food-borne bacteriological contamination should be taught in schools, colleges, and universities. Food safety should be a compulsory part of one's education.

Disease would be less frequent for certain if so.

Food-borne bacteria-germs are criminals, and go undetected because they are odorless, and can be airborne and waterborne, and scientists have estimated that each healthy person can share his or her body with more than 10,000 species of microbes, some healthy, some unhealthy.

They can grow and thrive, become super-toxic, carcinogenic, and cross-contaminate other foods at refrigerator and freezer temperatures.

They are responsible for food poisoning, disease, suffering, and death.

The problem with them is that they are so small that they can only be seen through a microscope. It would take 25,000 of some of them laid end to end to make one inch, and like humans, they consume food, give off wastes, and multiply.

Most viruses, pathogens, and parasites are contracted from person to person, either by handshake or touch, therefore personal hygiene is of the utmost importance.

We may not like to admit it, but humans are probably the greatest carriers and spreaders of germs. Humans carry more germs on their bodies than there are people on earth, and I am dismayed by those vague and ambiguous posted signs in hotel and restaurant bathrooms that inadequately state, "Employees must wash hands before returning to work."

The most grievous pet-peeve I have is that people who use a bathroom and leaves without washing their hands and exposed portions of their arms are guilty of contaminating toilet bowl flush handles, seats and lids, bathroom door handles, countertops, and whatever else they may touch, with traces of human feces or urine, thereby creating the killer bacteria E-Coil, which ultimately may cause illness and death to us all. It is infuriating!

I would like to see this filthy, despicable habit considered a serious crime, and at the very least, punishable by a heavy fine, and in the event of a death, a Federal offense, with the guilty party charged with being an accomplice to manslaughter.

Almost always, in every restaurant bathroom, that single, small, insignificant eight word sign is attached to the wall above the hand-basins, where every conscientious individual is already cleansing his or her hands, which is the absolute incorrect location for it to be.

The proper time to remind those unscrupulous, filthy-dirty individuals to wash their hands is when they are USING a urinal or bathroom stall, therefore, an advisory sign should be mounted on the wall at eye-level ABOVE each urinal, mounted at eye-level to the back of each bathroom stall door, directly on the wall or mirror at eye-level behind each hand-basin and faucets, and at eye-level close to the exit door of the bathroom.

Finally, there should be an additional sign mounted beside the bathroom exit door that reads: "In the interest of hygiene, please use a paper towel to open this bathroom door," with a waste basket for disposal of the paper towel close by.

Time and time again I have witnessed lamebrain, nitwit male slob scumbags use the bathroom and leave without washing their hands.

These advisory notices should be printed in bold black capital letters, in English, Spanish, French, German, Italian, and Japanese, (in order to reach international visitors) on white paper so they are clearly legible, and they should be either laminated or enclosed in a glass frame in order to eliminate defacing.

Our health protection laws are both inadequate and seriously lax in enforcement. Consequently, I suggest that what those weak-minded, unconvincing, and feeble bathroom signs SHOULD state is this:

Food Safety Hand Hygiene & Bacteriological Contamination Avoidance

· · · · · · · · · · ·

1. ALL foodservice employees (and ALL individuals) must wet hands and exposed portions of arms under warm running water.

2. Employees (and ALL individuals) must then scrub their hands and exposed portions of arms thoroughly with antibacterial hand soap and hot running water of at least 110 degrees Fahrenheit (43.3 degrees Celsius) for a minimum of 20 seconds.

3. Employees (and ALL individuals) must then rinse their hands and exposed portions of arms thoroughly with hot running water and dry them with a clean disposable paper towel, or hot-air dryer.

4. This procedure MUST be followed when employees are involved in the following, and before returning to work:
   (a) During food preparation to prevent cross-contamination when changing tasks.
   (b) After touching any part of the body other than clean hands and clean, exposed portions of arms.
   (c) Especially after bathroom use.
   (d) After coughing, sneezing, or using a tissue.
   (e) After smoking, eating, or drinking.
   (f) When switching between working with raw food, and working with ready-to-eat food.
   (g) After handling soiled equipment or utensils.
   (h) BEFORE putting gloves on for working with food.

5. These criteria are a zero tolerance company policy requirement, NOT a request, and ANY violation of this critically important company policy WILL result in the employee's IMMEDIATE dismissal.

Signed: "Management"

Perhaps some may consider these graphic words in a book about food to be offensive. To those who do, I would say, "GET REAL."

I am not concerned whether my remarks are offensive to someone. My aim is to attempt to bring awareness of this repulsive, loathsome, disgusting habit to the general public in an attempt to educate and correct those filthy half-brained nit-wits who don't cleanse themselves after bathroom use.

We need to keep pounding and pounding this into their stupid, foolish, naïve, absent-minded heads until they GET IT.

In my opinion all professional and domestic kitchens should be sterile, with professional kitchens designed to include a separate hand washing sink, with antibacterial soap, clean paper towels, or hot-air dryer, and hand sanitizer holders. The aroma of vanilla, spices, mint, lemon, or garlic is unquestionably pleasant to one's nose, but to me, the most important scent or odor emanating from any kitchen, professional or domestic, is that of a slight hint of vinegar or bleach water, indicating sanitary cleanliness.

For sanitary reasons, chefs should never wash their hands or exposed portions of arms in sinks used for food preparation, and anyone who works with food should be as conscious of bacteria, microbes, and cleanliness as a nurse or a doctor.

Unknown to most of the general public, European health codes correctly dictate that chefs and apprentices leave their aprons and hand-towels in the kitchen when going to the bathroom in order to avoid contracting bacteria on them while there, and then bringing it back into the kitchen.

When using a bathroom stall, chefs and apprentice jackets are removed, hung on a peg outside the bathroom stall, and not touched again until their hands and arms are properly washed. Also, at the end of each work shift in the kitchen, each chef is personally responsible for meticulously cleaning-up his or her station.

We can control "germs-bacteria" if we keep food covered, and keep perishable and prepared food in the refrigerator below 40 degrees Fahrenheit (4.4 degrees Celsius), and food which is to be served hot above 140 degrees Fahrenheit (60 degrees Celsius).

Cooking will kill germs, but may not kill the poisons they have produced. Therefore, eating this contaminated food may make a person very ill.

With food...especially with food, one cannot rest on one's laurels from previous accomplishments. One must be ever-vigilant in the fight against food-borne bacteria. Consequently the after-dinner mints and toothpicks offered at a restaurant's hostess counter should always be individually wrapped for sanitary reasons, and in an effort to prevent flies and other undesirable mites from contaminating perforated salt and pepper shaker caps, and sugar, grated cheese, oregano and hot pepper canister caps with larvae and intestinal deposits, these table items are best made available in individual paper packets.

Restaurants that do not use linen table-cloths should definitely use paper throw-away placemats for sanitary reasons. Additionally, for a server to wipe a tabletop with the same damp, pre-used, soiled cloth after each customer is simpleminded and unsanitary.

No live bird or animal should be permitted where food is prepared, stored, or served. Animals walk and feed on all kinds of filth, and can carry germs in on their feet, fur, bodies and mouths. Thankfully, in the late 1930's, antibiotic drugs were introduced to the world as a weapon in the battle against infection. However, more and more strains of bacteria have become resistant to the effects of antibiotics, meaning illnesses once treated with a regimen of antibiotics are much harder to control. Therefore, the best weapon of all against food-borne bacteria is strict cleanliness and sanitization.

Cleanliness equates success in a restaurant.

THE FOLLOWING IS A PARTIAL LIST OF THE MORE DEADLY KILLER BACTERIA, THEIR CAUSES AND SYMPTOMS. I BELIEVE IT SHOULD BE MANDATORY (IT IS NOT) THAT ALL CHEFS, YOUNG AND OLD, NO EXCEPTIONS, LEARN AND UNDERSTAND EACH ONE.

1. Norovirus
   Cause: The #1 cause of stomach flu. It is fast moving and highly contagious for 3 days to 2 weeks from contraction, and most prevalent at close quarters, i.e. cruise-ships, planes, stadiums, nursing homes, health - care workers, schools, toilets, food, water, and dirty hands.

   Symptoms: Diarrhea, vomiting and dehydration, stomach pain, flu symptoms.

   Treatment: Antibiotics do NOT cure. Constant, thorough hand washing with antibacterial soap and hot water is the best way to protect against this illness, moreso than using alcohol-based sanitizers.

2. E – Coli (Escherichia Coli) 0157: H7
   Cause: Foods that have come in contact with either human or animal feces. It has been found in raw clover, alfalfa sprouts, leafy lettuce, tomatoes, cucumbers, other produce, poultry, raw milk, other raw dairy products, raw meat products, and un-pasteurized apple cider. Triple washed greens can still contain E. Coli.

E. Coli. has been known to survive a sixty day ageing period in cheese.

Some leaner butcher, grocery store, restaurant, and meat processing plant cuts of beef, such as Sirloin, may have been mechanically treated by automated double-edged "blades" or "needles" in order to cut through tough muscle fibers and connective tissue in an effort to tenderize them for consumption. This process may contribute to a higher risk of E. Coli. poisoning if the machinery is not sterile, or if there were pathogenic organisms on the surface of the meat they would be pushed further into the muscle of the meat, thereby spreading the deadly bacteria.

Some grocery stores clearly label mechanically tenderized meat products, some do not.

All meats, especially ground beef or hamburger beef, whether mechanically tenderized or not, must be cooked to a minimum internal temperature of 160 degrees Fahrenheit (71.1 degrees Celsius), per U.S.D.A. recommendations.

All dairy products must be pasteurized.

Symptoms: Nausea, vomiting, bloody diarrhea, urinary tract infections, stomach cramps.

These symptoms can lead to a coma, anemia, kidney failure, hospitalization, blindness and death, especially for the very young, seniors, and persons with weak immune systems.

3. Salmonella Enteriditis
    Cause: Has been found in poultry, produce, eggs, dairy products. One in 20,000 eggs contains Salmonella.

    Symptoms: Fever, abdominal cramps, diarrhea.

4. Helicobacter Pylori (Also known as H-Pylori)
    Cause: Contracted through food and water.

Symptoms: Can cause gastric (Duodenum) pain, gastritis, peptic ulcers, stomach cancer, weight loss, appetite loss, burping, nausea, vomiting. Victim may obtain relief by eating food, drinking milk, or taking an antacid.

5. Shigella (Also known as Shigellosis)
    Cause: Found in water, food, salads, raw vegetables, milk, other dairy products, and meat.

    Symptoms: Mild abdominal discomfort to full blown dysentery, cramps, diarrhea, fever, vomiting.

6. Staphyllococcus / MRSA (Staph infection of skin)
    Cause: Has been found in beef, pork, chicken, turkey.

    Proper cooking kills Staph germs. MRSA strain is resistant to most antibiotics.

    Symptoms: Redness, swelling, pain, drainage of pus.

7. Listeria
    Cause: Usually found in cantaloupe melon, deli meats, hot dogs, chicken, soft cheeses, other dairy products, and has been known to survive a sixty day ageing period in cheese.

    It is more lethal than "Salmonella" or "E. Coli.."

    In pregnant women it can result in miscarriage, premature delivery, serious infection of the newborn, and stillbirth.

    Symptoms: Diarrhea, fever, muscle aches.

8. Campylobacter
    Cause: Usually found in poultry.

    Symptoms: Diarrhea, fever, vomiting, headache, muscle pain.

    It can be severe and life-threatening.

9. Toxoplasma
    Cause: Usually found in pork.

    Symptoms: Flu-like symptoms, muscle aches.

    Particularly dangerous to pregnant women.

10. Vibrio Vulnificus
    Cause: Found in raw shellfish especially raw oysters harvested from
    warm salty seawater in the Gulf of Mexico with temperatures of 81
    degrees F. (27.2 C) or higher, and warm brackish rivers and creeks
    from April to October. Pasteurization kills the bacteria.

    Symptoms: Diarrhea, vomiting and abdominal pain (cramping).
    V.V. is from the same family as Cholera, and the Centers for Disease
    Control (CDC) estimates the U.S. has about 4,500 cases of Vibrio
    annually.

    If medical treatment is not immediately obtained, it will (and has)
    cause death.

11. Botulism (Clostridium Botulinum) Types A.B.E.F.
    Cause: Usually found in swollen, bulging, or dented cans—tins of
    putrefied food, and foods showing signs of fermentation.

    Symptoms: Blurred or double vision, paralysis, nausea, respiratory
    difficulty, vomiting, diarrhea or constipation, cramps, sore throat,
    paresthesia, gastric pain.

    If left untreated by a doctor, it can cause death.

12. Dysentery (Travelers" Diarrhea)
    Cause: A result of viral, bacterial, protozoan infections, or parasitic
    infestations, these pathogens are the result of ingesting contami-
    nated food or water.

13. Hepatitis "A"
    Cause: An acute infectious disease of the liver caused by contaminated

food or drinking water. It is just one of several types of Hepatitis. It is highly infectious.

14. Typhoid
Cause: Typhoid is spread through contact with the stool of a person infected with the bacteria. This usually occurs by eating or drinking water that has become contaminated with feces from an infected person.

Typhoid is most common in Asia, Africa, Central and South America.

15. Cholera
Cause: Cholera is an acute diarrhoeal infection caused by ingestion of food or water contaminated with the bacterium "Vibrio Cholerae."

It affects both children and adults, and can kill within hours.

16. Ptomaine Poisoning
Previously believed to be caused by "Alkaloids" found in decomposing or decaying animal and vegetable matter which posses highly poisonous qualities. The term "Ptomaine Poisoning" was a general misconstrued, vague, and inaccurate term used before the actual causes of food poisoning were known.

This actual illness was most likely a bacterial infection from consuming contaminated food.

Symptoms: Diarrhea, vomiting, fever, kidney damage, and miscarriage.

• • • • • • • • • • •

• Hepatitis "B" has nothing to do with food.
It is contracted through blood, semen, and body fluids through sexual contact with an infected person, shared needles during drug use, being infected with HIV, transmitted from mother to child during birth, transfusion, or cut or break in the skin. It may lead to AIDS.

- Food service employees CANNOT contract AIDS by working or eating in a food-service environment with someone who has AIDS.

- Some types of poisoning can be caused by cooking or storing food in a galvanized container, or in a corroded dish containing zinc, copper, or lead.

- The elemental enigma of aluminum products and Alzheimer Disease has been theorized for decades; however, to date, scientists have determined that there is no clear evidence of the correlation of both.

Nonetheless, cooking with aluminum pots and pans should be avoided as a precaution.

It is almost impossible to avoid aluminum in our daily lives as it is an ingredient in toothpaste (Aluminum Oxide), public drinking, and bathing water (Aluminum Sulfate), powdered non-dairy coffee creamer (Sodium Aluminosilicate), antacids and aspirin (Aluminum Hydroxide or Glycinate), a leavening agent in baking powder (Sodium Aluminum Sulfate). therefore subsequently contained in self-rising flours, processed American cheese as a melting agent (Aluminum Salts), pickles (Aluminum Salts), and table salt as a free-flowing agent, and of course in aluminum pans and foil, soft drink (soda) cans, and aluminum wrapped chocolates or candies.

Molds on Food

Molds are microscopic fungi that live on plant or animal matter. Very much like icebergs, more fungi are hidden than are visible. No one knows how many species of fungi exist, but estimates range from tens of thousands to perhaps 300,000 or more. Most are threadlike organisms and the production of spores is characteristic of fungi in general. These spores can be transported by air, water, or insects. There are good and bad molds in fungi, and some penicillium species produce toxins that make food inedible or dangerous.

Spores give mold the color you see, and when airborne, the spores spread the mold from place to place like dandelion seeds blowing in the wind.

Molds have branches and roots that are like very thin threads which are poisonous. The roots may be difficult to see when the mold is growing on food and may have sprouted deep within the food. Foods that are moldy may also have dangerous invisible bacteria such as listeria, brucella, salmonella, and E-Coli growing along with the mold.

Some molds may cause allergic reactions and respiratory problems, and a few molds, in the right conditions, produce "mycotoxins," poisonous substances that can make people sick.

Mycotoxins are poisonous substances produced by certain molds found primarily in grain and nut crops, but are also known to be on celery, grape juice, apples, and other produce.

The Food and Agriculture Organization (FAO) of the United Nations estimates that 25% of the world's food crops are affected by mycotoxins, of which the most notorious are aflatoxins.

Aflatoxin is a cancer-causing poison produced by certain fungi in or on foods and feeds, especially in field corn and peanuts. Aflatoxins have been associated with various diseases, such as aflatoxicosis in livestock, domestic animals, and humans throughout the world, and the prevention of aflatoxin is one of the most challenging issues of the present time.

Molds tolerate salt and sugar better than most other invaders. Therefore, molds can grow in refrigerated jams, jelly, and cured salty meats.

Do not sniff moldy food. This can cause respiratory problems. If food is covered with mold, discard it.

Some imported and domestic delicatessen salami have a thin white mold coating, which is safe to consume. However, they should not show any other mold.

Dry-cured country hams normally have surface mold, which must be scrubbed off before cooking. Any cheese, whether hard or soft, including blue cheeses, that show signs of surface mold should be discarded.

Attempting to cut away the mold with a knife in an effort to save the interior of the moldy cheese can be counterproductive, as the knife may drag the mold and bacteria through the cheese and contaminate it. The only safe method of salvaging some of the cheese is to cut one (1) inch below and around the mold spot with a clean, sharp knife; otherwise, wrap it tightly in plastic and throw it out.

It is a prudent healthy policy to keep residential and commercial levels of humidity below forty percent (40%) in order to prevent the growth of mold within the premises.

Water

Water is our most precious element. We cannot survive without it.

I have placed it high on the list because of its immeasurable importance to us.

It is essential to all forms of life. Our water supply purity and security is our life's blood.

Water is a colorless transparent liquid, tasteless and odor-less. It is a compound substance of two portions of weight of hydrogen with one of oxygen (hence the term h2o).

Water freezes at 32 degrees Fahrenheit (F) = 0 degrees Celsius.

Water boils at 212 degrees Fahrenheit (F) = 100 degrees Celsius.

One (1) pint of water weighs one and one quarter (1&1/4) lbs.

One (1) gallon of water weighs ten (10) lbs.

One (1) cubic foot of water weighs sixty-two-point-three (62.3) lbs. (1,000 oz)

One (1) ton of water equals two hundred, twenty-four (224) gallons.

At altitudes above 3,000 feet, lower air pressure causes differences in the boiling point of water.

At 39.2 degrees F. (approximately 4 degrees C.) pure water has its highest density (weight and mass): 8.34 lbs / gallon.

It covers over 70% of the earth's surface, and 30% of all fresh-water courses through the ground.

Surface water bodies (lakes, rivers, brooks) make up only 0.3% of the total fresh-water on earth (or 1/150 of 1% of earth's total water supply).

Sixty-eight-point-seven percent is frozen in ice caps, glaciers, and permanent snow in Antarctica and Greenland.

Some public water utilities have been found to contain contaminants and toxins to include pharmaceutical and industrial chemicals.

The Environmental Protection Agency (EPA) regulates municipal drinking water quality for the presence of approximately 90 to 100 toxins, setting maximum safety levels for drinking water contaminants like arsenic, fluoride, nitrates, lead, and coliform bacteria in city water.

These bacterial contaminants and toxins are not detectable in drinking water, and very small concentrations of them can cause kidney, liver, and nervous system damage, along with learning disabilities, and diseases such as typhoid, dysentery, cholera, hepatitis, and giradiasis (water-borne parasite).

A recent U.S. Geological survey (1991–2004) revealed that 34% of private wells tested positive for E. Coli, or total Coliform bacterial contamination.

Use of an ultra-violet (UV) light inactivates harmful bacteria, viruses, and pathogens in private well water.

Reverse Osmosis is a method of restoring beneficial minerals. It raises pH to a more natural level, and improves the taste of water.

Installation of a charcoal filter on one's kitchen faucet significantly reduces the amounts of many pollutants, and may also improve the quality and taste of municipal and private well water. Unfortunately, bottled drinking water companies do not remove many contaminants, and the delivery of un-refrigerated bottled water at fluctuating temperatures while on the delivery truck may allow bacteria to grow in the bottles before it reaches the unsuspecting public marketplace. Bottled water should ALWAYS be kept refrigerated at 40 degrees F. (4.4 degrees C.) or lower, and never left in heat or sunlight, as this will aid in the growth of bacteria.

Drink bottled water only from a refrigerated, unbroken, sealed bottle, especially in tropical locations. Do NOT use ice cubes unless you KNOW they are made from a non-contaminated source of drinking water.

Society requires….indeed DEMANDS…safe drinking water supplies, for our own sake, and that of our children, and those who will follow us.

Milk

Milk is a white alkaline liquid produced by the mammary glands of mammals.

There are no poisonous elements in milk. In fact, because of lactic acid and digestive juices, milk is a valuable internal antiseptic.

Normally, milk is easy to digest, especially for children. However, persons who cannot digest milk lack an enzyme in their system called Lactase. This is called 'Lactose Intolerance" (see chapter on Food Allergies and Intolerances).

Milk is about 87% water. The other 13% is made up of solid particles, protein, butterfat, carbohydrates, vitamins, minerals, and trace elements.

Milk contains calcium (for bone health), phosphorus, sodium, potassium, chlorine, sulfur, iron, copper, zinc, aluminum, manganese, iodine, magnesium, vitamins B-2 (riboflavin), B-l, B-6, B-12, and is credited with reducing mild hypertension and selected cancers.

It is considered one of the most perfect foods in nature, more a food than a drink.

Of the 13% solid particles, nearly one-third is very high quality protein. It contains all of the essential amino-acids the body needs to build tissue.

Bodybuilders once considered milk necessary for bulking up, then were told "Milk will make you fat," so most abandoned milk as a part of their diets. However, some still recommend it as a bulking food for young body builders trying to develop outstanding physiques. Milk is not carbohydrate- rich, with only 1.5 grams per ounce, so it is not the best fuel for hard training sessions.

Nonetheless, milk does contain approximately four percent butterfat and cholesterol, and it has been associated with cardiovascular disease.

The butterfat content of whole milk includes Lecithin and Cepholin, as well as fat-soluble vitamins A, D, E, and K.

A cup (8 fluid ounces) of whole milk contains 160 calories, compared to a cup (8 fluid ounces) of non-butterfat milk, which contains 85 calories.

The three common forms of reduced-butterfat milk are:

A. Low-fat milk of two percent butterfat content or less.
B. Low-fat milk of one percent butterfat content or less.
C. Non-fat or skim milk, with a butterfat content of close to zero (0. l) percent.

Before Louis Pasteur (see * below), all milk was consumed in its "raw" state, which made it very dangerous to drink. Unpasteurized milk can carry "salmonella dublin," an intestinal infection that spreads to the bloodstream, causing illness and death.

At the turn of the 20th century, U.S. scientists discovered a link between "raw" or "bad" milk and Microbacterium Tuberculosis (known as T.B. Disease), a disease which is spread through the air from one person to another, attacking any part of the body including the lungs, kidneys, spine, and brain, and can be fatal if not treated properly. So, in 1907, U.S. scientists were successful in making the pasteurization of milk the law in the U.S., and as a result dramatically slowed the progress of T.B. among the population.

It is good, sound advice to avoid drinking raw, unpasteurized milk.

Evaporated milk is pasteurized whole milk with 50 percent water reduction, homogenized, with vitamin D added, and then sterilized. It is unsweetened.

Sweetened condensed milk is evaporated to reduce its water content by 40 to 50%, with sugar added.

Homogenized milk is mechanically treated to blend the butterfat globules throughout the milk. Milk freezes at 30 degrees Fahrenheit above zero (minus 1.1 degrees Celsius).

The "tepid" point of milk is considered "lukewarm."

The "scalded" point of milk is considered "just below boiling."

The "boiling" point of milk is approximately 214 degrees Fahrenheit (101 degrees Celsius) depending on altitude and atmospheric pressure. Skim milk boils quicker because it is mostly water.

Bovine Spongiform Encephalopathy (BSE), also known as "Mad Cow Disease," is a disease in dairy cows that gradually eats holes in the animal's brain.

A key part to U.S. human safety is that the animal tissues that can carry the B.S.E., including the brain and spinal cord, are removed from cattle before they're processed for food.

The World Health Organization says humans cannot be infected by drinking Pasteurized milk from cows with B.S.E.

* A French chemist and microbiologist, (born December 27, 1822 – died September 1895), inventor of the first vaccines for rabies and anthrax, and who proved the theory that germs come from germs, and who, as a consequence, invented and in 1873 patented, the process of Pasteurization in the U.S.

Pasteurization is the process of slowing microbial growth in liquids such as milk, wine, and beer, by heating them to 160 degrees Fahrenheit, (71.1 degrees Celsius) for a minimum of 15 seconds, and then cooling them to 50 degrees F. (10 degrees C).

Monsieur Pasteur was awarded the National French Legion of Honour for his incredible contributions to society.

Butter

Butter is the fatty globules extracted from fresh or fermented cream by churning.

Its origin dates back to the early nomadic people.

Butter can be made from the milk of cows, ewes, she-goats, mares, she-donkeys, and she-camels.

U.S. law mandates that commercial butter must contain at least 80 percent butterfat, and according to the American Heart Association, butter has less trans-fatty acids (artery-cloggers) than margarine. European butter has a higher butterfat content of 83 percent.

Butter tastes best at room temperature, and its incomparable flavor in cooking is immeasurable. Properly wrapped in foil or plastic, butter can be frozen in its original wrapper for up to nine months, then thawed without too great a change in flavor or texture. Tightly wrapped butter can be refrigerated for several weeks.

The melting point of butter is 86 degrees Fahrenheit (30 degrees Celsius).

Butter may de-salted by soaking, squeezing, and rinsing in a bowl of iced water until it feels smooth and waxy, then shaping and patting to remove all extra water.

The two most famous butters in my opinion are the French "Beurre de Bretagne" (Brittany Butter) and the Irish "Kerrygold," (from grass to gold).

Brittany butter is produced in the Finistere region in the extreme west of France.

It is almost always flecked with large, coarse grains of French-Celtic salt harvested from Atlantic seawater off the coast of Brittany, France, which gives it a slight crunch and shimmer when bitten into.

27

Unlike the rest of France, "Bretons" sometimes butter their bread, which is only done elsewhere in France with Oysters and Rye bread ("Pain de Seigle").

The word "Amann" is the Breton word for butter.

"Kerrygold" is the world famous creamery butter made at small family dairy farms whose cows graze in lush green pastures in Ireland's heartland.

It has a distinctive, creamy taste and texture, especially during the summer months when the Kerrygold cows' milk is most abundant in naturally softer milk-fat. This softer milk-fat results in a velvety smooth pure butter. "Kerrygold" butter is exported from Ireland worldwide.

Important Butter Compositions

• • • • • • • • • •

"Compound Butter"
Butter mixed with one or more pureed or chopped substances such as garlic, chopped shallots, herbs, fungi, cooked shellfish, leafy and fresh vegetables, nuts, spices, mustards, lemon zest and juice, and used as flavoring for vegetables, seafood, meat, soups, sauces, and various other dishes. It is then rolled and wrapped in wax paper and refrigerated or frozen until ready to use.

"Maitre d'Hotel Butter" (Used with meat, fish, boiled vegetables)
Blend butter with chopped parsley, freshly ground black pepper, and a dash of lemon juice.

"Bourguignonne or Escargot Butter"
Blend butter with chopped shallots, crushed garlic, chopped flat-leafed parsley, sea salt, freshly ground black pepper, and a dash of brandy or dry white wine.

"Caviar Butter" (Used for canapes, Hors d'oeuvre, and with seafood)
Pound the caviar in a mortar with butter and pass it through a sieve.

"Homard (Lobster) Butter"
Pound cooked lobster coral in a mortar, add butter, and pass through a sieve.

"Truffle Butter"
Pound small truffles in a mortar, add Bechamel Sauce and butter, and pass through a sieve.

"Beurre Manie" (Kneaded Butter)
A compound of 5 tablespoons (75grams) of butter and ¾ cup (100grams) of plain flour blended into a smooth paste. It is then used as a quick liaison to bind certain soups and sauces.

"Clarified Butter" (Clear Butter)
Heat butter on a very gentle beat until melted. A whitish deposit (milk) will form on the bottom of the saucepot. Gently strain the clear, transparent butter through a muslin cloth into another container. Or, reduce the butter over a slow heat until the milk content has evaporated and the butter is clear in color.

"Beurre Blanc" (White Butter)
Simmer chopped shallots in wine vinegar for 1 hour, adding a little dry white wine if it becomes too dry. Strain this reduced liquid into a small saucepan and briskly whisk in diced butter over a high heat until the sauce becomes thick and smooth.
   Do NOT allow the sauce to separate.
   Add lemon juice, salt and freshly ground white or black pepper.

"Beurre Noisette" (Nut-brown Butter)
Melt and cook butter past the "clarified" stage, and until the salt content turns a nice, light brown, hazelnut color.

"Beurre Vert" (Green Butter)
With a mortar and pestle, pound raw spinach, parsley, watercress, and chopped shallots together. Place them in a cloth napkin and extract the juices. Strain the juice through another cloth napkin placed over a small bowl. Add this juice to softened butter with capers, French mustard, lemon juice, salt, and freshly ground black pepper. Wrap it

into a roll in wax (greaseproof) paper and refrigerate, or freeze it until ready to use.

"Beurre Rouge" (Red Butter)
With a mortar and pestle, pound cooked shellfish carcasses and 1 tablespoon of paprika together and add butter. Transfer the mixture into a saucepot and very slowly melt it.

Strain the mixture through a muslin cloth and allow it to chill.

Wrap the butter into a roll in wax (greaseproof) paper and refrigerate or freeze it until ready to use.

"Beurre Noir" (Black Butter)
Melt and cook butter past the "Noisette" stage until it turns black. Strain, and add one tablespoon white wine vinegar, one tablespoon finely chopped parsley, and one tablespoon capers.

"Citrus Butter"
Combine one tablespoon of orange and lime zest, 1½ tablespoons grapefruit juice, and four ounces of butter until well blended. Serve with seafood or grilled chicken.

"Beurre Chantilly"
Melt and add cognac and red wine and whip over an ice-bath.

"Butter cream"
Beat softened butter with a whisk until creamy; add sweetening and flavoring and use for filling and decorating tortes, cakes, and pastries.

If refrigerated, butter-cream will turn smooth again when brought to room temperature and re-whipped.

Cream cheese is sometimes added to enhance the taste, and if so, and it is to be kept at room temperature, it should be consumed within one to two hours.

Sugar, Honey, Stevia

Sugar

White table or granulated sugar (sucrose) is derived from sugarcane (a giant grass), and sugar beet (a root).

Its use in cooking is monumental, as it is used by chefs from soup to nuts.

Studies have shown it to be linked to obesity, diabetes, cardiovascular disease, dementia, macular degeneration, and tooth decay. Other studies have shown no evidence of sugar causing cancer, and further clarification on these studies remains inconclusive. Clearly, diet and exercise remain the best offense against these diseases. The recommended caloric daily intake of sugar for men is 150, and for women 100. Brown sugar is cane sugar containing varying amounts of molasses, depending on whether it's light or dark.

Confectioners (powdered) sugar is granulated white sugar crushed and sifted to a desired fineness, or powder.

Cube sugar is granulated white sugar pressed into square molds.

Maple sugar is the product remaining from evaporating maple tree sap or maple syrup.

Date sugar, either the "medjool" or "hallawi" variety, is 80 percent sugar, and (since it contains the date fiber) is considered by scientists to be the healthiest sweetener with no adverse effects on human blood sugar, thereby earning it the moniker "the ideal food."

Honey

The nectar of flowers and plants that is gathered, concentrated, and stored by honeybees is the most beneficial substitute for sugar. This sweet, delightful, golden-colored, easily digested energy booster has been utilized since the ancient days. Honey consists of glucose, water, and fructose along with several vitamins and minerals.

Its most ideal medical application is for a sore throat, as it has the power to kill the bacteria that is the main cause for throat infection.

Honey can be used to treat or enhance the following: allergies, stomach ailments, blood purification, bowels, skin, sleep sedative, and of course its immense importance in everyday and high level cooking.

Stevia

A natural herbal sweetener, Stevia is a genus of many species of herbs and shrubs in the sunflower family, and some of the extracts may leave a bitter or licorice aftertaste. It is purported to have up to 300 times the sweetness of sugar.

It has been known for centuries as a sugar substitute; however, the U.S. banned Stevia in the early 1990's UNLESS it was labeled a dietary supplement.

Stevia was approved for use in Europe in December 2011.

Stevia was introduced in Japan as an alternative to "Cyclamate" and "Saccharine," which were suspected carcinogens, and Japan now accounts for 40 per-cent of the sweetener market.

Eggs

The versatile egg has reigned as one of our basic foods from the beginning of human history.

Eggs are one of the most important and basic elements in anyone's kitchen.

They are nutritious, containing vitamins A, B6, B12, Riboflavin, Iron, and Magnesium, and of course are economical.

We depend on the egg for aristocratic, rich, creamy soufflés, cakes, pastry, meringues, crepes, pancakes, custards, batters, quiches, pasta, binding croquettes, nogs, salads, garnishes, sauces such us Zabaglione, Mayonnaise, Hollandaise and Bearnaise, omelets, and just plain boiling, sautéing, scrambling, poaching, baked-en-cocotte (shirred eggs), and use of the white and the shell to clarify consommé and jellies.

An egg is an emulsifier and a natural leavener, which means it holds fats and water together in salad sauces and several other recipes.

Recent studies have determined that the cholesterol from an egg yolk (approximately 215 milligrams) does not raise a person's blood cholesterol to the degree that saturated fats do.

American Egg Nutrition Board scientists estimate that only one of every 20,000 eggs produced in the U.S. contains the bacteria Salmonella Enteriditis.

Nonetheless, chefs and consumers should exercise caution as the risk of serving certain people (such as the elderly, the very young, pregnant or nursing women, and people whose immune systems have been compromised by medical treatment for AIDS or cancer) is very high and the consequences of contamination are very bad. A single contaminated egg would be all it took for someone in one of those risk groups to get life-threateningly ill.

1. Buy only clean UNCRACKED grade A or AA eggs. Never use eggs whose shells are cracked.
2. Keep eggs refrigerated at 40 degrees Fahrenheit, 4.4 degrees Celsius, or below. Eggs have a maximum room temperature shelf-life of only two hours to be safe from bacteria.
3. Eggs should be stored in their cartons in an upright position on the narrow pointed end of the shell, never on the wider round end or on the sides. The narrow pointed end is the hardest part of the shell; the wider round end contains an air cell which should be undisturbed. Place carton on a middle shelf of the refrigerator not the door, as it opens constantly, subjecting the eggs to varying temperatures.
4. Eggs hatch at 104 degrees Fahrenheit above zero (40 degrees Celsius).
5. Fresh egg shells are rough and chalky, old eggs are smooth and shiny, and the coarse, granular shell of an egg has more than 17,000 pores, which allow the egg to "breathe," but also prevent bacteria from invading it.
6. To determine whether an egg is fresh, immerse it in a pan of cool, salted water. If it sinks, it is fresh; if it rises to the surface, it is stale, so throw it away. Also, when cracked open, the yolk of a fresh egg should stand-up near the center, be firm, and cling to the white. The older an egg gets, the flatter the yolk becomes, and the runnier the white gets.
7. To determine whether an egg is uncooked or hard-boiled, spin it. If it spins, it is hard-boiled. If it wobbles and will not spin, it is raw.
8. Egg whites will cling tightly when poaching if you add a little white vinegar to the water.
9. Eggs will beat up fluffier if they are allowed to come to room temperature before beating.
10. For baking it's always best to use medium-sized eggs.
11. Egg shells can easily be removed from hard-boiled eggs if they are quickly rinsed in ice-cold water first.
12. For fluffier omelets, add a pinch of cornstarch before beating.
13. For never-fail meringues, add a pinch of salt, ¼ to ½ teaspoon of cream of tartar, and a tiny drop of blue coloring to the egg whites (and the sugar of course).

14. Grease or fat is egg whites worst enemy when making meringues.

15. To prevent egg shells from cracking, add a pinch of salt before boiling.

16. Brush beaten egg white over pie crust before baking to yield a beautiful glossy finish.

17. It is a myth that brown-shelled eggs are better than white shelled eggs. The color of an egg shell is determined by the breed of the bird, and has nothing to do with the quality of the egg.

18. When a recipe calls for the use of half an egg, beat the egg thoroughly and divide it in half.

19. Egg yolks should be tempered by blending them with cream for use as a "liaison" thickener in sauces, and after incorporation, the sauce should NEVER boil again or it will curdle.

20. When a recipe calls for the addition of several eggs, break each one into a small soup cup and add them one at a time. This prevents spoiling the entire recipe by adding a bad egg. Also, occasionally an egg will have a "blood" spot, which should be removed prior to use.

21. Always wash hands, utensils, equipment, and work surfaces with hot soapy water after preparing eggs.

Flour

Flour is modern roller-milled from wheat kernels (grains), which is composed of three separate parts: 84% endosperm (inner core), two percent germ (embryo / seed), and 14% bran (hard outer shell).

The bran and germ and all their natural nutrients, fiber, protein, calcium, iron, and minerals, are removed, and the endosperm, containing complex carbohydrates and gluten, but absent those natural nutrients, is ground and sifted to make white flour, which is then enriched with synthetic chemical vitamins and minerals.

When first freshly milled, white flour is a yellowish color, but if left to age naturally for approximately 10 to 15 days, it eventually becomes an off-white color. To speed the whitening process, bleaching chemicals are added. This bleaching process is only done in the U.S. and it is illegal in Europe as it is considered toxic to do so. Because it is quickly digested in the human body, bleached white flour spikes blood sugar, is high on the glycemic index, and is known to cause heart disease, high cholesterol, and weight gain.

There are three main types of white wheat flour, along with several other varieties. The white wheat flours include:

1. Bread flour, made from winter wheat and high in protein, enables dough to rise well and bake to a firm texture.
2. Cake flour, the most highly refined flour, made from soft wheat, has low protein, resulting in a crumbly texture.
3. All-Purpose White Unbleached flour, a compromise of the two, has medium protein content, is used for bread and cakes. Unbleached flour is not infused with Potassium Bromate.*

Other varieties of flour include:

- Enriched bleached flour (contains Azodicaronamide, also used in foamed plastics).
- Self-rising flour (made from soft wheat with leavening and salt added, then bleached and enriched).
- Wholemeal (100% wheat grain), wheatmeal (80% wheat grain), wheatgerm (has an extra 10% of wheatgerm added).
- Buckwheat flour (made from finely ground buckwheat kernel).
- Pastry flour (is less finely milled than cake flour, made from soft wheat).
- Rice flour (milled from rice).
- Rye flour (milled from rye grain for bread making).
- Soy-Bean flour (milled from soybean).
- Graham flour (unbolted from ground wheatmeal kernels).
- Instant type all-purpose flour (dissolves quickly in liquids without forming lumps).

In the U.S. some bread manufacturers dye white flour brown to make it look like "Whole Grain," and there are no stipulations or regulations to prevent this.

Flour should be stored in small quantities in a glass or heavy plastic jar or tin, in a cool dark cupboard at a maximum of 75 degrees Fahrenheit (23.8 degrees Celsius) or cooler for six to eight months, (Wholewheat flour for two to four weeks), or in the refrigerator or freezer for up to 18 months. Flour that has been frozen should be thawed before use. Unprotected stale or out-of-date flour will lose moisture and dry out, can turn rancid, become insect infested, or will grow mold and may impart an unpleasant flavor.

* Potassium Bromate

• • • • • • • • • •

Potassium Bromate is an oxidizing enhancing agent used to strengthen and improve flour in the U.S., Great Britain, and Japan. It is banned in the rest of Europe, China, and other countries throughout the world. This compound is also used in hairdressing permanent – wave solutions.

Its purpose is to cause flour to "bulk-up" and make bread rise quicker.

The International Agency for Research on Cancer has labeled it a category 2-B carcinogen. It has been linked to cancer in laboratory animals, and has also induced tumors in rats in a 1982 research study.

It is NOT banned in the U.S., and the Food and Drug Administration (FDA) has taken no action to restrict its use as an additive to flour, although they have urged bakers to stop using it, and the American Bakers Association (ABA) says most of its members have ceased using it.

The State of California has required the use of a warning label about it on flour packaging.

U.S. law does NOT require it to be listed as a separate ingredient on food labels. Consequently, you will not find it listed on supermarket flour packages.

I encourage readers to further research this product to their own satisfaction.

Salt

There are two types of salt—rock salt and sea salt.

Rock (iodized table) salt is mined from the earth in crystal form, then refined, at which time most minerals are removed from it until it is pure sodium chloride.

Regular iodized rock (table) salt and sea salt are almost the same chemically.

Both contain approximately 98% of sodium chloride, ounce for ounce, (2,300mg. per teaspoon). Iodized salt is table salt mixed with a minute amount of potassium iodide, sodium iodide, and a small amount of dextrose to stabilize the iodine.

Iodine is important in preventing thyroid hormones (lypothyroidism), which can cause goiter, cretinism in children, and myxedema in adults.

In European countries where water fluoridation is not practiced, fluoride salts are added to table salt.

Sea salts have been harvested from ponds and marshes since the seventh century, and there are upwards of 50 to 100 of the fine, glistening crystal and flake varieties scattered throughout the world.

The more elite sea salts are known as "Finishing Salts." Finishing sea salts are unrefined. Therefore, it is imperative that the water supply it comes from be free from undesirable pollution. They have a residual moisture content reaching upwards of 10%. Because of their higher cost, it is important that you understand how to use finishing salts. Considered an artisanal product, finishing salts should only be sprinkled on a dish by the chef just before serving, and should never be nonchalantly used during the cooking process.

The true, most revered, and most expensive finishing salt, sometimes called "White Gold," and the "Caviar of Salts," is Fleur de Sel de Guerande.

It reigns supreme, and is the premier artisan sea salt composed of young, white-gray crystals that form naturally on the surface of salt evaporation marshes and ponds in Brittany on the North-West coast of France.

Paludiers (salt rakers), and Sauniers (salt workers), using the Celtic method of wooden rakes (as no metal should touch the salt), usually only hand-harvest it during the hottest three months of the year.

Fleur de Sel de Guerande contains calcium, magnesium, potassium, iron, zinc, manganese, and other trace minerals like sodium chloride.

Other notable French finishing sea salts are Fleur de Sel de Ile de Re, Fleur de Sel de Camarque, and Fleur de Sel de Ile de Noirmoutier.

The Mediterranean island of Cyprus produces a luxurious, white, snowflake-type artisan sea salt. The Pacific Ocean island of Hawaii produces sea salts that are pink and black. A natural mineral called alaea (volcanic baked red clay) is added to enrich the salt with iron oxide.

Australia produces a rose-colored sea salt from Murray River, Victoria, in South-East Australia. Italian sea salt is produced from the low waters of the Mediterranean Sea along the coast of Sicily. It is a natural salt rich in iodine, flourine, magnesium, and potassium, and has a much lower percentage of sodium chloride than regular table salt.

Kosher salt is used in the preparation of Jewish dietary guidelines. It generally comes in flakes rather than granules. Kosher salt is not necessarily sea salt.

Coarse salt is a larger-grained sea salt. Chefs use it for salt crusts on fish and meats (en Croute de Sel).

Grinder salts are large dry crystals used in salt mills. Always use a salt mill with a ceramic or plastic grinding mechanism. Metal, including stainless steel, will corrode, and will taint the salt's flavor. Some parallel sea salts are:

England: Maldon Sea Salt, from Blackwater Estuary, Essex, England.

Spain: Flor de Sal d'Es Trenc, from Ses Salinas, Majorca (considered Spain's answer to the French Fleur de Sel), and Flor de Delta.

Portugal: Flor de Sal from Aveiro, and Flos Salis from the eastern Algave.

Phillipines: Pangasinan.

Thailand: dork gleua from Samut Sakorn.

Vietnam: Shinkai, an exotic pearl deep-sea salt.

Korea: Bamboo Salt, which is roasted in bamboo containers and mud, between 800 and 2,000 degrees Centigrade (1, 472 and 3, 632 degrees Fahrenheit).

Iodized salt is prepared with the addition of Iodine.

Gray (rock) salt contains traces of valuable minerals such as arsenic.

Celery salt is fine salt flavored with dried and powdered celery.

Do not salt fried food immediately after frying it; it draws out water and makes the food soggy. It is preferable to salt it at the table.

Bath salts contain unrefined raw sea salt, and is used for therapeutic effects.

In humid environments and conditions, one should add a few grains of uncooked rice to salt shakers to absorb extra moisture.

Sodium is one of the primary electrolytes in the body.

On March 12, 1930, Mahatma Ghandi led 78 barefoot protesters (eventually ballooning to thousands, and lasting 23 days), who made their own salt from the sea, on a 240-mile non-violent march to Dandi, India, in protest of paying a salt tax to the British Empire. This civil disobedience elevated the Indian independence movement from an elitist struggle to a national struggle to its eventual independence achieved in August, 1947.

Salt is regarded by some as the "silent killer," as it attacks the kidneys, therefore chefs and cooks should use it sparingly in cooking. However, salt enhances flavor in sweet things, strengthens gluten and lengthens shelf life in bread, and cutting it from recipes won't remove much sodium from one's diet.

Nonetheless, we should try to restrict our intake of sodium chloride (salt).

Lemons

Lemons play an integral part of cuisine for any chef in the kitchen, from lemonade and limoncello, gremolato and lemon curd, to syllabub (a thick lemon-orange, cream, sugar, and sherry drink), to lemon juice used to acidulate water for bleaching apples, pears, avocado, and artichokes, preventing them from turning brown when left exposed to air. Lemons are regarded as a chef's best fruit friend.

Lemons add acid, which can heighten other flavors, and a bright, tangy flavor to foods.

Lemons are full of vitamin C, folate, fiber, and potassium.

Almost all lemons sold in North America are either a Eureka or Lisbon variety. These lemons are similar, oval in shape, and bright yellow inside and out.

A much smaller Meyer lemon crop comes from California, Arizona, and Florida.

Meyer lemons are a thin-skinned, round citrus fruit native to China, sweeter than regular lemons, with a beautiful orange floral aroma. They are not as acidic as regular lemons.

Rising culinary interest by chefs means they are increasingly available at markets.

Unlike regular lemons, their harvest is limited from December through May.

In Sicily, Limoncello (lemon flavored vodka) was invented in the early 1900's using Sorrento lemons, the zest of which has a high content of lemon oils.

Limoncello may be kept in, and served from, the freezer.

1. A good, juicy Eureka or Lisbon lemon should be small, firm, smooth-skinned, and without heavy blemishes.
2. To get the most juice out of fresh lemons, before squeezing, roll them at room temperature under the palm of your hand against your work surface, applying pressure with you hand.
3. Lemon juice is a natural antibiotic, tonic, diuretic, and restorative and will soothe and whiten the skin and lighten hair. It is also a non-toxic cleaner, softener, and deodorizer.
4. Persons with gout or rheumatism should NOT use lemon juice because of its acidity. However, a teaspoonful in a glass of warm water has been used to bring down fevers in illnesses such as typhoid, and helps induce sleep.
5. The acid from the juice of half a lemon prevents crystallizing when making caramel sauce.
6. When just a few drops of lemon juice are needed, pierce the skin at one end with a needle or skewer to puncture in a few places, and squeeze the desired amount.
7. Before cutting a lemon in half for squeezing, grate the zest, but never the bitter white pith beneath. Then store it in a tightly covered container in the freezer until you need an amount for a recipe.
8. Lemon zest (peel) is good for fevers as it helps induce sweating.
9. Tightly seal a completely grated, whole lemon in plastic wrap, and store in the refrigerator until lemon juice is needed.
10. The deeper yellow color a lemon is, the less acidic it is likely to be.
11. A few drops of lemon juice added to the water when boiling rice will prevent it from sticking.
12. Use lemon slices in your iced drinking water for a refreshing taste.
13. Whole lemons will burst if you freeze them. However, lemon juice freezes very nicely. Use an ice-cube container.
14. Discard, and don't buy, any lemon with a soft, spongy patch. It's an indication of interior decay, and will soon turn moldy.
15. Some samples of lemons as a garnish: Lemon peel twists, half lemon flowers, lemon "baskets," fan-shaped slices, scored lemon slices, half a lemon with a pig's tail twist of the rind, caramelized lemon halves.
16. Lemon grass is one of the most important ingredients in Asian cooking. It is a reed-like plant that grows as a thin, firm, two-foot stalk with a small bulb at the base. It varies in color from pale yellow

to very light green. It has a pleasantly assertive lemon taste and aroma, and is used in simmering, and finely sliced or chopped in almost any meat or seafood dish. When simmering, use only the bottom six inner inches of the stalk, pound it with a meat mallet until well bruised in order to release the flavor. Strain and discard before serving. The bulb and bottom two inner inches may be cut julienne or diced, cooked, and served with the dish.

17. Keep a squeezed-out lemon half by the kitchen sink to rub on your hands in order to kill odors after handling strong-smelling foods like fish, garlic, onions, or to remove food colorings.

18. Rub cloudy glass coffee pots, pitchers, or decanters with a cut lemon to add the sparkle back to the glass.

19. To clean plastic or wooden cutting boards, rub them with a cut lemon half, rinse, and air dry.

Herbs

There are so many aromatic herbs that to try to list them all in this minor work would be almost impossible.

Herbs, especially fresh herbs, are absolutely essential to fine cuisine.

Fresh herbs are always very mild. Dried herbs are more concentrated in flavor. Dried herbs have about twice the strength of fresh herbs, and should be used in half measure to fresh green leaves. Use both varieties sparingly until you have become accustomed to their effects in cooking. It is much easier to add extra seasoning, rather than attempt to subtract seasoning.

Bay leaves are the exception. You can use the same amount, fresh or dried.

The best method of drying fresh herbs is to tie them in bunches and hang them in a well-ventilated space out of direct sunlight in a maximum temperature of 80 degrees Fahrenheit (26.6 degrees Celsius). Another method is to microwave them at high for five minutes. They should then be allowed to cool before storing.

Dried herbs should be stored in airtight glass or pottery jars in a dark, cool cupboard. The maximum storage time is approximately one year.

To refrigerate fresh herbs, wash and wrap them in a paper towel and place them in a plastic bag. They will stay fresh for one week.

Fresh herbs may be frozen in small, plastic freezer bags or airtight containers. If freezing fresh basil or dill, first blanch in a bundle in boiling water for 10 seconds, then plunge into iced water to refresh and retain their bright green color. Frozen herbs will keep for approximately one year. Thawed herbs cannot be successfully re-frozen.

Do not wash fresh herbs until you are ready to use them.

When chopping fresh herbs, especially Genovese basil, the knife must be very, very sharp, otherwise it will crush the basil, oxidizing it, and it will then turn black. With fresh Genovese basil, it is preferable to tear it apart with your hands at the very last minute.

Most fine European hotels and restaurants maintain a fresh herb garden normally located somewhere to the rear of the building, and if the establishment is large enough, one or more full-time gardeners are employed to weed, till, and provide the kitchen with fresh herbs and vegetables daily. In some cases, first-year apprentice chefs are tasked with tending to the herb garden.

The Ten Most Important Herbs Essential to Fine Cuisine

• • • • • • • • • • •

1. Parsley: Curly parsley is used for decoration. Flat-leaf or Italian parsley is used for flavor.
2. Basil: There are several varieties of basil, including chocolate, lemon, and cinnamon, just to mention a few. Use Genovese basil raw on tomatoes and salads, and only add it to cooked dishes just before serving.
3. Oregano: Delicious on pizza, and tomato based dishes.
4. Rosemary: Usually paired with fish, lamb, and pork.
5. Cilantro: Also known as Chinese parsley, it is used in Asian and other dishes around the world.
6. Thyme: Used in soups, stews, casseroles, and marinades.
7. Sage: Excellent with poultry, pork, and other meats.
8. Chives: A member of the onion family, it is flavorful in sauces, and as a garnish.
9. Dill: Mostly used in pickling, but very good with eggs, vegetables, and potatoes.
10. Mint: Flavors of mint include peppermint, pineapple, ginger, spearmint, and more. It may be used in desserts, drinks, meats, and vegetables.

Saffron

Saffron is the most expensive spice in the world. Its list price was once set on the Philadelphia commodities exchange equal to that of gold. Its top grade is called "Coupe" saffron.

The stamen of the cultivated saffron crocus, which grows from a bulb (or corm), and only flowers in mid-Autumn, blossoming at dawn, usually produces three vivid crimson stigmas (or stamen) approximately one inch in length, which must be quickly and tediously plucked, piled, and dried by hand.

The bloom window for the stigma is within one to two weeks, with October regarded as the optimum point to collect, when it is believed to be at its apogee.

Originating in the bronze-age in the East and introduced into Spain by the Arabs, it has been cultivated in France since the sixteenth century. It is considered indispensable by French chefs in the preparation of Bouillabaisse, a classic Marseilles seafood dish which legend says was not created by Venus, the goddess of love, but rather by the abbess of a Marseilles convent for a Friday abstinence meal.

Pure saffron contains more than 150 volatile and aroma-yielding compounds, and should be a dark orange color throughout.

The dried stigmas have been widely used throughout the world for centuries, mainly in various cuisines as a seasoning and coloring agent, and give a golden-yellow-orange hue to dishes such as rice, noodles, vegetables, poultry, lamb, fish, desserts, Italian Risotto alla Milanese, and the incomparable Marseilles Bouillabasse.

Saffron is grown and produced in the drier regions of Bihud, Iran (which accounts for 90% of global production), Spain, Portugal,

Greece, France, Austria, England, Germany, Switzerland, Morocco, New Zealand, Kashmir-India (this variety has a dark, maroon-purple color), by the Pennsylvania Dutch in Lancaster County, Pennsylvania, in San Gavino Monreale-Sardinia, and the premium quality "Zafferano dell'Aquila" grown in the Navelli Valley of Italy's Abruzzo region near L'Aquila.

Its enemies are rabbits, rats, and birds, who cause damage by digging up the crocus corms. It takes an acre of land and hundreds of thousands of flowers to produce one pound of saffron threads. Roughly 150 flowering plants yield but one gram (0.035 oz.) of dry saffron threads. It takes 0.45 kilograms (1lb) of saffron threads to yield 0.2 oz. of dried saffron, and one kilogram (2.2lb) of saffron stamen yields 12 grams (0.42oz) of dried saffron.

Dry saffron is highly sensitive to fluctuating pH levels and rapidly breaks down chemically in the presence of light. It must therefore be stored away in air-tight containers in order to minimize contact with atmospheric oxygen. Saffron is somewhat more resistant to heat.

The dried threads of saffron should be soaked in hot, but not boiling, water for several minutes prior to use in cuisine. This helps release the beneficial components.

Although it is a dry product, it should be used within two years of its production date, as the natural oils it contains tend to dry out beyond that time period.

Pure saffron should not be confused with substitutes such as Safflower, (known as bastard saffron, and sometimes sold as "Portuguese Saffron," or "Annatto" (poor man's saffron), also called Roucou, and is a natural plant extract used as a spice, and a dye in red food coloring, textiles, and body care products such as lipstick. Its identification number is E160b when not specifically listed by name on food products. Another herb commonly confused for saffron is turmeric powder, a spice known as "Indian Saffron," which is derived from the root and rhizome of the Curcuma Longa plant. This product of India, which is reddish in color and has an acrid and bitter flavor, and smells slightly of ginger and saffron, is used mainly in curry powders and yellow mustards.

Cleopatra used saffron in her warm baths, believing its perfumed fragrances contained an aphrodisiac that would enhance her lovemaking.

In Europe in the middle ages, those found selling adulterated saffron were executed.

Truffles (Truffe)

Truffles are a subterranean, edible, aromatic, and piquant fungi, of which a number of varieties exist, growing three to twelve inches deep in the soil mostly beneath oak trees, but also under birch, willow, elm, and aspen. Their exact location is a closely guarded secret by local farmers.

There are two types of truffle: black (Black Diamonds) and white.

The most highly esteemed black truffle (Truffee Noir), comes from Perigord, France.

Truffles are also gathered in Dauphine, Burgundy, Normandy, Lot Valley, and Vacluse, France.

White truffles (Truffes Blanches) come chiefly from Piedmont, in the north of Italy. They are, however, also found in North Africa and in some regions of France. Not surprisingly, the Piedmont variety remains the most valued because of their aroma and texture, and costs as much as three times the cost of the French Black Perigord.

A winter crop, growing from about mid-December until the end of February, they are not easy to find, and are traditionally hunted every eight days or so beneath wintry snow, leaf mold, and moss by young sow pigs (who will, if allowed, eat the truffles), and mongrel dogs (who disdain the aroma and will immediately drop them).

When unearthed, they are of course covered in mud and are usually golf-ball to baseball sized.

Sometimes a farmer may find truffles on his own, because flies swarm over where the truffles lay buried beneath a truffle oak tree.

Once gathered, truffles should remain covered in soil. Otherwise, if exposed to air, they begin to lose their flavor and perfume.

To clean truffles, use only a soft brush, toothbrush, or toothpicks to remove the soil. NEVER wash them in water.

A common practice is to then store them in containers of dry rice until needed for presentation. The aromatic rice may then be cooked and served. The black truffle is usually cooked in pork fat that has been simmered slowly and then passed through a fine strainer.

The white Piedmont truffles are predominantly eaten raw, sliced thinly, and used as garnish just before serving.

Recently, cheap, immature, unripe, tasteless Chinese truffles have been flooding the world's markets, and in fact are being processed and packed in France, and legally sold as "Product of France."

There is no comparison whatsoever in taste to the French truffle.

Caviar

Wild caviar is the roe, or raw eggs, of a large fish, especially sturgeon, mainly from the Caspian Sea, but also from the Black Sea, and harvested and produced by Russia and Iran between March and April (the peak season).

The sturgeon is usually caught at breeding time, when they transfer from deep ocean waters to shallow riverbeds in order to spawn. The roe at this time is oily and unsuitable to the palate, so the sturgeon is caged and starved so they will purge themselves of the excess oil.

The sturgeon roe only becomes caviar after it is carefully cleansed and meticulously salted to perfection. Consequently, there is no unsalted caviar.

The native Russian term for caviar is "Ikra."

The English word caviar is derived from the Turkish word "Khavyah," which in turn is derived from an Iranian-Persian dialect. It was first introduced into Italy, and named "Caviala" around 1300 A.D., and from there further introduced to the rest of Europe and the western world.

A single large Beluga sturgeon can produce up to 125 pounds of roe.

A single Osetra sturgeon can produce approximately 35 pounds of roe.

A single Sevruga sturgeon can produce approximately seven to eight pounds of roe.

All caviar is colored gray-black. However the color is no indication of quality.

Per 100 grams, caviar contains 270 calories, 25.3 grams protein, 17 grams fat, 440 mg cholesterol, four grams sugar, 1,700 mg sodium, 164 mg potassium, 330 mg phosphorus, 51 mg calcium, vitamins D, A, C, B2, B44, B12, and PP.

Caviar must be kept tightly covered and refrigerated between 34 and 36 degrees Fahrenheit (1.1 and 2.2 degrees Celsius), and should be removed from the refrigerator 15 minutes before the meal in order for the aromas to reconstitute.

Caviar should NEVER be frozen, as it will liquefy and become mushy.

Caviar must always be tasted either via a horn, bone, wood, gold, or mother-of-pearl cutlery. SILVER CUTLERY SHOULD NEVER BE USED, as it alters the taste of the caviar.

For those who find the taste of caviar too strong, caviar may be spread thinly on Melba toast or small Blini pancakes topped with a hint of chilled crème fraiche, or sour cream.

White Russian vodka is the perfect accompaniment. However, dry champagne is also delicious with caviar.

Beluga (sturgeon), known as "Malosal" (little salt), has the highest quality and is the most highly prized caviar because it has the biggest eggs. The egg color varies from light gray to nearly black. It is incredibly rare, and less than 100 fish per year are now caught in the Caspian waters, representing barely one per cent of the sturgeon catch.

Because it is considered an endangered species, Beluga caviar has been prohibited for interstate trade in the U.S.A. since 2007.

Osetra (sturgeon) caviar from the Caspian Sea has a distinct, almost gorgeous nutty taste, and many connoisseurs consider it to be the best caviar.

It is golden-brownish in color, and sometimes slate gray.

Sevruga (sturgeon) caviar is the smallest, and has the strongest flavor of all sturgeon eggs, which are gray-black in color, with a fine grain. Sevruga sturgeon is more plentiful, consequently its eggs are less expensive.

Paiusnaya (pressed) caviar is saltier than Malosol, but nonetheless a highly prized finished delicacy.

Keta (red caviar) is made from salmon roe.

Whitefish or lumpfish caviar is originally yellow-green in color and later dyed with charcoal.

Processed, non-refrigerated caviar sold in 1oz. and 5oz. glass jars has a shelf life of only three months.

Malosol (Beluga) caviar is an exceptional, delicious item and must be tasted according to precise rules and protocol, and to a true connoisseur, must be served in its original box on a glass or plain white china or porcelain plate, always encircled in crashed ice, and unadorned by any accompaniment other than Melba toast, or small Blini. This precious pearl of kings needs no enhancement.

Accompaniments such as pepper, lemon, onion, chopped egg white and yolk, unsalted butter, parsley, or other herbs are usually served with lesser quality caviar as a garnish.

Vanilla Bean

On the rich, fertile, red soil on the North-East coast of the island of Madagascar, which lies 250 miles off the coast of Mozambique (Southern Africa) in the Indian Ocean, vanilla bean farmers laboriously cultivate what is regarded as the world's gold standard of vanilla bean.

Other tropical locations such as South America and Mexico, which produces the flavorful "Vanille de Ley," also help satisfy the world's appetites and demands for the vanilla bean.

This versatile, aromatic member of the orchid family is an Epiphyte, which is an air-plant (not planted in the ground) that attaches itself and grows on another larger tree in order to benefit from a higher level because it needs to reach sunlight in order to survive.

This is known as a symbiotic relationship, meaning it is advantageous to both species. Only one vine per tree is the rule.

If allowed, it can grow as high as 30 to 40 meters (98ft. to 131 ft.) high, which would make it almost impossible to harvest by hand. Consequently, farmers prevent that from happening by gently removing the plants tentacles from the tree with a long, forked branch.

The first orchid flower, which is not very bright in color, takes three to five years to bloom. The bloom does not have nectar, so therefore the birds and bees are not drawn to it. Consequently, it must be pollinated by human hand using a toothpick-like pointed twig or stick to transfer the pollen from male to female flower.

The vanilla flower only opens-up once, usually in March, at approximately 7:00 a.m., and closes at approximately 11:00 a.m. and each bloom produces only one vanilla bean per flower.

The bean is difficult to identify as it blends in almost exactly with the vine it grows on. Once picked green from the plant, the beans must be placed in plastic bags and cured in the sun in one day for only two hours in the morning. They will turn a very dark brown color.

The drying process takes six weeks at two hours daily for each vanilla bean, after which it must undergo a sweating and drying process every other day for six weeks, and finally, a condition and aging process for a further three months. From start to finish, the whole complex and tedious process takes between nine to 10 months to harvest and complete, usually beginning at the end of October or early November through January/February and sometimes into March.

Pure vanilla extract (essence) is made with alcohol (usually 41%), vanilla bean extractives and water, and is a gluten-free food.

The best method for storing vanilla beans is in a glass, air-tight jar in a dark place. The taste will simply get stronger with age and the beans will last forever (or at least for 50 years). To use a vanilla bean, place it on a clean, flat surface, trim both ends, cut along ONE side of the bean and open it up. Hold the knife at a 45-degree angle and using the back of the knife, scrape at least 10 times to remove all the thousands of tiny seeds (known as vanilla caviar).

Do not waste or throw away the outer fibrous husk as it is also loaded with flavor. It can be returned to the glass jar for use later in custards and sweet sauces, or soaked in a glass of water overnight, rinsed and chopped or pulverized in a high-speed blender for mixing into ice cream or puddings.

Hopefully now you have a greater appreciation for the high cost of the amazing aromatic pure vanilla extract (essence).

Do not purchase or use imitation products as they can NEVER compare to the real thing.

Yogurt

To make yogurt, take some milk, add the bacteria "Lactobacillus bulgaricus" and "Streptococcus thermophilus," and allow it to ferment in a warm place until it thickens. It can then be covered and refrigerated.

In order to retain all of yogurt's "good" bacteria (Probiotics, or "live and active cultures"), it should be enjoyed cold, or at room temperature.

NEVER heat it!

Yogurt contains animal protein, calcium, vitamin B-2, B-12, potassium, and magnesium.

Persons who are lactose intolerant should eat yogurt with few or no ill effects.

The live bacteria cultures in yogurt destroy lactose.

Live, living, or active cultured plain yogurt is successful against osteoporosis (calcium deficiency in bones), fighting off colds, hay fever, diarrhea, cataracts, cholesterol, and may assist in lowering rates of breast cancer in women.

While on vacation in foreign countries, eat yogurt instead of other dairy products to help prevent "travelers diarrhea." Infection-causing pathogens can't thrive in it as they do in milk and other foods.

Frozen yogurt lacks the "good" bacteria of regular plain yogurt, and will not give you the same health benefits.

Outdated, mold-contaminated yogurt should be discarded.

Four Renowned Blue Cheeses

Most cheese is made from the milk of three main sources: cows, sheep, and goats. However, cheese may be made from any milk-secreting-mammalian-animal such as camels, mares, Asian water buffalo, reindeer, etc.

In some cases, some of the finest cheeses are blends of two, or all three of the main milks.

Cheese contains proteins, calcium, phosphorus, vitamins A & G, and is one the most digestable foods.

Since I am an aficionado of the blue variety of cheese, I have chosen to write only about the four most celebrated blue cheeses: the French Roquefort, Italian Gorgonzola, Danish Blue, and the English Stilton.

Three of these four blue cheeses are manufactured with the introduction of P. Roqueforti (Penicillium Roqueforti) spores, (French Roquefort, Danish Blue, and English Stilton), and the fourth with Penicillium Glaucum (Italian Gorgonzola), and are perfectly safe to eat.

Also, several different Penicillium species are used in making cheese, and the Penicillium molds used in cheese making do not generate the drug Penicillin, and therefore pose no problem to anyone allergic to the drug.

The Asian water buffalo mentioned above lives and grazes in the southern part of Italy known as the boot. It is different from what we call the American Buffalo, which in fact is not a buffalo, but a bison.

The U.S. Food and Drug Administration (FDA) requires ALL cheese, domestic or imported, to be made from milk pasteurized by being heated to 145 degrees F. (63 degrees C.) for thirty minutes, or

161 degrees F. (72 degrees C.) for fifteen seconds, and the cheese must be aged for at least 60 days at a temperature no lower than 35 degrees F. (1.7 degrees C.).

Pasteurization rids cheese of bad bacteria such as Listeriosis, and Brucellosis. Therefore, cheese made with raw (unpasteurized) milk should be avoided.

Although some cheeses have the flexibility to be served before dinner, in France, cheese is served after the main course, not before it. I am in agreement with this concept as I believe hors d'oeuvre especially are supposed to stimulate the appetite, not dull it.

In Italy, cheese is sometimes served with slices of fresh pears or apples in place of dessert.

In England, cheese is generally served after dessert.

The perfect partner for cheese is wine, and professional wine tasters are forbidden to eat any cheese between sips, as it may give the wine superior nobility.

Do not freeze natural cheese, and when serving, bring cheese to room temperature to maximize flavor and normalize texture.

Garnish cheese with slices of ripe fresh pears, sweet apples, figs, or red seedless grapes. Traditionally, blue veined cheeses are served at room temperature with port after the meal, or as a dessert only.

I personally like any blue veined cheese with watercress, figs, and hazelnuts.

French Roquefort

• • • • • • • • • •

Regarded by most elite cheese connoisseurs as "the king of cheeses," this artisan cheese is made from the milk of Lacaune, Manech, or Basco-Bearnaise ewe sheep in the limestone Mont Combalon caves of Roquefort-Sur- Soulzon, in the South of France.

In 1961 French law decreed that only this blue cheese was permitted to bear the name Roquefort. It is aged and ripened for five months, and its distinctive veins of blue-green mold give it its nuances of an intense sharp, damp earth, and salty tang.

It has no rind, and the exterior is edible.

The blue-green mold culture (Penicillium Roqueforti) in Roquefort is achieved by adding molded white French breadcrumbs (no crust), through holes poked through the exterior. These molded breadcrumbs may only be produced in the natural caves of Roquefort-Sur-Soulzon.

There are only seven Roquefort producers who hold access to a cave for the production of the mold process in the cheese.

Roquefort has a high content of free glutamate, 1280 mg. of free glutamate per 1000g. (3.5oz). The best wines to accompany Roquefort are: any red Bordeaux, Bourgogne, Chambertin, Cote du Rhone, Hermitage, or Chateauneuf-du-Pape, and champagne of course!

Danish Blue (Danablu)

• • • • • • • • • •

Made from cows' whole milk, it is a strong, sharp, salty, blue-veined cheese with an edible rind.

It is aged eight to 12 weeks, and before ageing, copper wires or rods pierce the formed round drum to distribute the mold Penicillium Roqueforti evenly throughout the cheese.

Holes made by the copper rods can be seen when the finished cheese drum is cut.

Italian Gorgonzola

• • • • • • • • • •

Made from unskimmed cows' and/or goats' milk, it is mainly produced in the northern Italian regions of Piedmont and Lombardy.

During the ageing process, metal rods are quickly inserted and removed, which creates air channels, and spores of the mold Penicillium Glaucum are added into the air channels and are then allowed to grow, causing its characteristic dark-blue veining.

If adding it to risotto it must be melted into it in the final stage of cooking and should only be used with short pasta such as penne and rigatoni etc, not with spaghetti, linguine, angel hair, or lasagna.

Chef Patrick J. Gorey

English Stilton

• • • • • • • • • •

There are two types of Stilton cheese: blue and white.

English Stilton is produced from pasteurized local cow's milk in the counties of Derbyshire, Leistershire, and Nottinghamshire to a strict, protected designation of origin European Commission code, which surprisingly does NOT include the village of Stilton, Cambridgeshire, where the first Stilton was made, and is named for.

Its distinctive, slightly-bluer-than-Roquefort veins are created by piercing the crust of the cheese with stainless steel needles, allowing air into the core, when Penicillium Roqueforti is added into the blue variety only.

It takes approximately 12 weeks to produce and ripen, and the rind is edible.

Olive Oil

A collection of facts and interesting nutritional, and healthful information about the benefits of one of our most versatile, succulent, and delectable ingredients.

This passionately crafted, intense, exquisite, robust, aromatic, and velvety light green shimmering essence with such rich heritage is so revered in Italy, it is known as "Olio Santo" (Holy Oil).

There are four basic presses from olives, two cold and two heated.

The first cold press is known as extra virgin (used for bread dipping, drizzling salads, vegetables, pasta).

The second cold press is known as virgin (also known as pure olive oil or olive oil).

The first heated press is known as classico (also known as lampante or light). It has a smoke point of 438 degrees F., and is good for sautéing.

The second heated press is known as pomace (also known as extra light). It has a smoke point of 468 degrees F., and is good for stir frying and deep frying.

An olive begins life green in color, then changes to beige, then to purplish brown, and its texture softens as the oil content increases. Since they are too bitter to eat uncured, olives need to be cured in brine, salt, or lye. Once covered in brine or olive oil, they can last indefinitely. The pasteurization of olives for bottling virtually cooks and renders them mushy. Consequently, the best tasting olives are those that are cured and unpasteurized.

Olive trees were first discovered around 2,500 B.C. in Crete, Greece, and Syria, and olive oil has survived between three and six thousand years throughout the Mediterranean region.

Each olive tree lives between 300 and 600 years, and when an olive tree dies, it regenerates itself. New roots emerge around the base and grow into a new tree.

In ancient Greece, harming an olive tree was a capital offense, and the olive tree was so revered that anyone caught cutting one down was put to death.

The average olive tree yields 40 pounds of olives a year.

It takes 10 pounds of Olives to make one liter of olive oil.

Olive oil has four enemies: age, heat, air, and light.

Olive oil is 77% monounsaturated fat, 9% polyunsaturated fat, 14% saturated fat (the highest level of Monounsaturated fat of any oil).

Olive oil has NO cholesterol or salt. It contains 120 calories and 14 grams of fat per tablespoon.

Olive oil's main component is oleic acid…which reduces bad cholesterol, or LDL (low density lipoprotein), and triglycerides. Olive oil maintains good cholesterol, or HDL (high density lipoprotein). However, monounsaturated fat will ONLY lower cholesterol if it RE-PLACES saturated fat in one's diet.

It also prevents hypertension by reducing blood pressure and is beneficial in reducing the risk of coronary heart disease, colorectal and breast cancers through the regulation of cholesterol.

Cold pressed olive oils are the only *unrefined* oils on the market. Unrefined oil retains its polyphenols (Vitamins E & A…powerful antioxidants).

Rub olive oil on your skin *after* sunbathing; it could help reduce the risk against skin cancer and wrinkles, enabling you to look and feel better. Take two teaspoons of extra virgin olive oil thirty minutes BEFORE a meal to act as an appetite suppressant. (Mix with a dash of good Balsamic Vinegar for variety)

Classico, (or light) olive oil still contains fat and calories…"Light" in this instance does NOT mean less of either.

Do NOT heat or refrigerate extra virgin olive oil as it will lose its robust flavor (Refrigeration will cause it to become cloudy).

For flavored olive oil, add fresh herbs of your choice, cap tightly and store in a cool dark cupboard for six weeks.

Always buy small "estate" bottles of olive oil which have a harvest date, for faster use (thereby eliminating the possibility of rancidity).

Olive oil is a five-billion dollar business annually.

Italy is Europe's largest importer and exporter of olive oil, and Italian law states that as long as an olive oil is *packed* in Italy, it can be labeled, a "Product of Italy."

The absence of an abundance of French olive oil is the result of continual freezing temperatures in Provence in 1956 and 1985. Some small olive farmers never recovered.

Olive oil freezes at 36 degrees Fahrenheit above zero (approximately two degrees Centigrade).

Olive oil MUST be stored in a tightly capped bottle in a COOL, DARK cupboard, and if so will have a shelf life of one to two years (no sunlight or Ultraviolet rays).

It has been said that to taste extra virgin olive oil is like kissing God.

Olive Oil Baking Conversions

• • • • • • • • • •

Butter ******		Olive Oil ********
1 teaspoon	equals	¾ teaspoon
1 tablespoon	equals	2 & ¼ teaspoons
2 tablespoons	equals	1 & ½ tablespoons
¼ cup	equals	3 tablespoons
1/3 cup	equals	¼ cup
½ cup	equals	¼ cup plus 2 tablespoons
2/3 cup	equals	½ cup
¾ cup	equals	½ cup plus 1 tablespoon
1 cup	equals	¾ cup

Escargots (Snails)

Escargot is the French word for snails.

These juicy, tender mollusks are perfectly safe morsels to eat when prepared properly. They are high in protein and low in fat content. However, when cooked and served in a Bourguignonne (Burgundy) butter, they disprove that theory.

Normally served as an appetizer as opposed to an entrée, they are high on the list of gourmet French dishes. Nonetheless, it is a myth that all French people enjoy escargots.

Not all species of land snails are edible. The common garden slugs without shells are inedible.

Snails are hermaphrodites; both are male before and during mating. After mating, they both become female. They normally couple for 12 hours.

In springtime, maturing takes approximately three months. In Autumn, it takes approximately nine months. Birds, mice, and snakes are their enemies.

It is a fact that if you whistle at a snail while it is still in it's shell, it will emerge.

Free-range garden snail farming in Europe is booming, where Escargots are tremendously more popular than in the U.S., and there is a European Commission which monitors their production. Also there are organic free- range snail farms throughout the world, which, to be successful, must have a natural setting with good soil, natural air circulation (achieved with chicken-wire enclosed pens), evening dew or moisture, vegetation such as fresh growing spinach, garden lettuce, clover, carrots, sage (or other fresh herbs for flavor), and correct nutrition (calcium, sodium) in order for them to grow rapidly.

During long, hot days, snails seek shade on the underside of plant leaves and the most opportune time to harvest them is immediately after a rainfall.

After harvesting, snails cannot be eaten right away. They must first be cleansed of their fecal matter, placed on a strict clean diet (no vegetation), and fed a second clean diet to plump them before they reach the final sizzling aromatic presentation at the dining table. Consequently, the following steps must be adhered to:

1. To harvest snails, they must only be collected using a canvas or paper bag (no plastic), or if using a bucket or pail, then it must be covered with a breathable cloth (no lid) in order to allow them to continue to breathe.
2. After harvesting, place them in a wire or cloth-covered container (plastic is acceptable) with a handful of either cornmeal or semolina for three days in order to purge them of the intestinal impurities in their digestive systems.
3. Repeat this procedure a second time.
4. Transfer them into another clean, cloth-covered container and starve them for an additional three days, all the time allowing them to breathe. During this period they will operculate — retreat and seal themselves into their shells, become dormant and hibernate, which is perfectly normal. Remove them and wash them in a colander, allowing excess debris to pass through. During this washing, they will awaken from their slumber. Remove and discard any dead snails.
5. Lay remaining snails on a tray, open side up, and sprinkle them with sea salt to induce mucous, then place them in a fifty per-cent white vinegar and water bath to purify them. Drain, and again rinse them under cold running water in a colander.
6. Plunge the snails into a pot of vigorously boiling water for five minutes to kill them.
7. Drain, cool, and remove them from their shell in order to trim and discard the bottom of the body known as the foot.
8. Prepare a Court-Bouillon (fish stock), with a Bouquet-Garni (Fresh herb combination) and white wine, or a fifty per-cent beer and water combination, and simmer for one to three hours (depending on the size of the snails).

9. In order to purify the shells, they should be boiled separately in water and sodium-bicarbonate (baking soda) for 30 minutes, rinsed in cold water, and dried.

10. To serve, snails must be replaced back into their shells, and the shell and snail filled and topped with Bourguignonne butter (butter, chopped garlic, diced shallots, flat-leaf parsley, freshly ground black pepper, sea-salt, and a dash of brandy or dry white wine), dipped in fine dry breadcrumbs (to keep them moist while baking), placed on an indented metal plate, the crumbed side up, and baked on a tray in a 400 degree F. (205 degree C) oven for approximately five to eight minutes until sizzling.

11. Finally, they should be served with one or two slices of garlic toast (to dip into the snail butter), and an escargot tongs (to hold the shell, as it will retain heat), and a cocktail or escargot fork.

Pre-cooked, canned Escargots should be rinsed and drained of their liquid, and placed in a shell with Bourguignonne butter, baked and served as above.

The perfect accompaniment for escargot would be either a sweet, fruity white wine or champagne.

Gold and Silver

It is somewhat of a myth that gold and silver are inedible.

Embellishing foods with precious metals is a centuries old tradition that originated in the East, where silver was believed to be beneficial for the liver and to possess aphrodisiac qualities.

The edible gold most commonly used today is similar to the tissue-thin gold leaf (1/200,000 inch thick) used on picture frames or free antique French furniture.

This gold leaf can be purchased in booklets of 25 3 3/8 inch square sheets.

The U.S. Food and Drug Administration considers these miniscule amounts nontoxic as long as the gold is within the 23 to 24 karat range.

A lower karat count could potentially be harmful because additional metal alloys are present.

It is preferable to purchase from museum suppliers rather than art-supply stores, which may carry lower- karat varieties.

As a former Chef Patissier, I have used gold-leaf extensively, although mostly on chocolate torte, chocolate truffles, and chocolate art display pieces for buffet tables.

Some famous epicureans have used it with lobster, caviar, truffles, poached flesh pears, and even demitasse coffee.

Edible silver-leaf and silver-dust is more popular in the East, where it is sometimes used on kabobs and special rice dishes.

Aahh…the Midas touch!

The Menu

The word "menu" means "bill of fare," "carte," "small," "slender."

It is a sheet of paper, cardboard, or chalkboard on which is written, in specific order, the names of all the dishes which are to be served in succession at a given meal.

In olden French times, it was called an "escriteau." (bill of fare)

The first true bills of fare as we now know them originated in France around 1850 when owners of inns and the first true restaurants began the tradition of presenting individual menus to all restaurant clientele in the belief that they should have the right to choose the dishes that most pleased them. Once French restaurants started presenting guests such menus, the custom caught on everywhere.

Chefs at prestigious restaurants adopted the habit of placing large posters (called escriteau) near the entrance of their restaurants, and on these were written the names and, sometimes, descriptions of dishes provided by the establishment.

English visitors to France liked the idea so much that before long, every pub in London had a chalk-board upon which the pub owner would list his daily offerings. The French, in turn, liked this English adaptation and most Parisian restaurants began to use chalkboards for the same purpose.

Until the middle of the eighteenth century, most public eating places were inns—places where overnight guests or others who dropped in could have a meal. No matter how plain or fancy these places were, the contents of the meals to be served were determined by the proprietor or the kitchen staff, and every guest was given exactly the same thing to eat. If there were menus in such establishments, they were hung over the working stations in the kitchen and were solely for the purpose of the chefs or cooks. In most such inns, not even the waiters knew what the dinner would consist of until they were given the various dishes to bring to the table. It is true that by the middle of the seventeenth century, waiters in better French, English, and Italian inns and hotels were told what dishes would be served, and it was the responsibility of one of the waiters to memorize this list and announce loudly to all the assembled guests just what was waiting for them.

During the last half of the 19th century, many restaurants outdid each other in trying to make their menus artistic and elaborate, some of them embossed with gold and bound in silver.

Famous artists did not consider it beneath their dignity to illustrate such menus, and menus embellished by Toulouse-Lautrec, August Renoir, Henri Matisse, and Paul Gauguin have now become highly prized collectors items.

Sometimes the artists would receive payment for their work, but more often they would accept meals in return. Renoir prepared menus for his favorite restaurants and it is rumored that after the age of 35 he never again paid for a restaurant bill. Toulouse-Lautrec, who was a respected gourmet, agreed to sketch menus for those restaurants to which he was invited to dine on the house.

The most expensive to prepare and the earliest known menu was discovered by archaeologist Sir William Cristal in 1922 when he was excavating the pyramid that contained the tomb of a then unidentified Egyptian prince. Carved in hieroglyphics on stone tablets, the menu was for the meal that was presented to celebrate the birth of the prince's twin sons, one of whom was to later become Ramses III, probably the most powerful and famous of all Egyptian pharaohs.

The hieroglyphic tablets, now on permanent exhibit at New York's Metropolitan Museum of Art, are valued at millions of dollars.

The famed French dean of chefs, Fernand Point, observed that "every menu has three purposes: to please the eye, to trigger the appetite, and to advise people how much of their money they are about to spend." The most important function "is that of pleasing the eye and the other senses," said Point, "for if the menu is not appealing, the people will lose their appetites and their desire to part with their money."

The composition of a perfect menu should be accurate, concise, harmonious, short, and absent of spelling or grammatical errors. Do not be guilty of composing deplorably lengthy menus if you do not have sufficient staff to produce them successfully. Know your limitations.

Menus should be spotlessly clean. Food spots and torn or crushed pages on the menu make customers wonder whether the kitchen is as dirty as the menu they have just been presented with.

When menus have become dirty or otherwise unattractive, they should be discarded. A menu should be changed with the seasons in order to take advantage of seasonal produce and products, and a menu must never repeat itself. For example, no two items of the same make or color; also it is more elegant to not use the dollar sign with the price, nor end the price in pennies.

Avoid using "a la" more than once on the menu.

In restaurants that list their daily offerings on a chalkboard it is perfectly legitimate to cross out one of the dishes when it has been sold out. Restaurants that have a printed menu do not have this privilege, and it gives a very bad impression when items have been crossed out with a pen or magic marker. If you have run out of a specific dish on a certain day, the waiter should state this when he presents the menu.

If certain dishes have been eliminated permanently from the menu, the menus should be reprinted. Little pieces of white paper pasted over the names of dishes that used to exist make a restaurant look inept.

Menus should clearly show whether a gratuity is included in the prices. Customers who discover when they receive their bill that their meal is going to cost 20% to 25% more than the menu prices are going to be angry people.

Angry people do not return, and will refrain from recommending the restaurant to their family or circle of friends.

The French word hors d'oeuvre means "outside the meal." The word should always remain in the singular, and should never be written on a menu in the plural. Hors d'oeuvre should be light, hot or cold, appetizing tidbits served prior to a meal.

The first thing I ask for when I consult with restaurateurs is the menu. Invariably it is written like a novel, and therefore takes much too long to provide prompt, efficient service, which inevitably results in a dissatisfied customer who may not return, and again, will not recommend the restaurant.

Chefs should always sign their menus along with their title, in order to convey their pride in their craft to their guests.

All artists sign their creations.

The following are some advisories which may be considered for placement at the bottom of restaurant menus:

- Please inform your server of any food allergies, sensitivities, or food intolerances.
- Gluten-free, lacto, ovo, and vegetarian dishes available upon request.
- Please be aware our kitchens use peanuts, tree nuts, eggs, shellfish, fish, milk, soy, and wheat. While we take many steps to prevent cross-contamination, there is always the potential that it may occur.
- Consuming raw, undercooked, or partially cooked meats, poultry, seafood, shellfish, eggs, or unpasteurized milk may present a health risk to the consumer and may increase your risk for food-borne illness, especially if you have certain medical conditions.
- There is a risk with consuming raw oysters. Chronic illness of the liver, stomach, or blood, or an immune disorder, has a greater risk of side effects from raw oysters. If unsure, consult a physician.
- Please refrain from the rude use of cell phones in the dining room (failure to respect this rule will result in your expulsion from the restaurant).
- No cigarette, cigar, or pipe smoking allowed on any part of the restaurant property.
- We are committed to the comfort and ambiance of our dining facility, the efficiency and friendliness of our staff, and your satisfaction.
- We take great care to make your dining experience a pleasant experience.
- We always use the finest and freshest ingredients available, and we grow and cultivate our own herb garden without pesticides.
- If for any reason you do not receive the maximum in service and courtesy from our employees, we appreciate your letting us know.
- We proudly operate a clean, bacteria-safe environment.

- Yes, we have a kids' menu. If that doesn't work, we'll be delighted to offer something different for your children. Just ask your server. We love our valued younger customers.
- Our recommended healthy, extra virgin olive oil is served free upon request.
- This happy establishment is proudly , independently family-owned and operated.

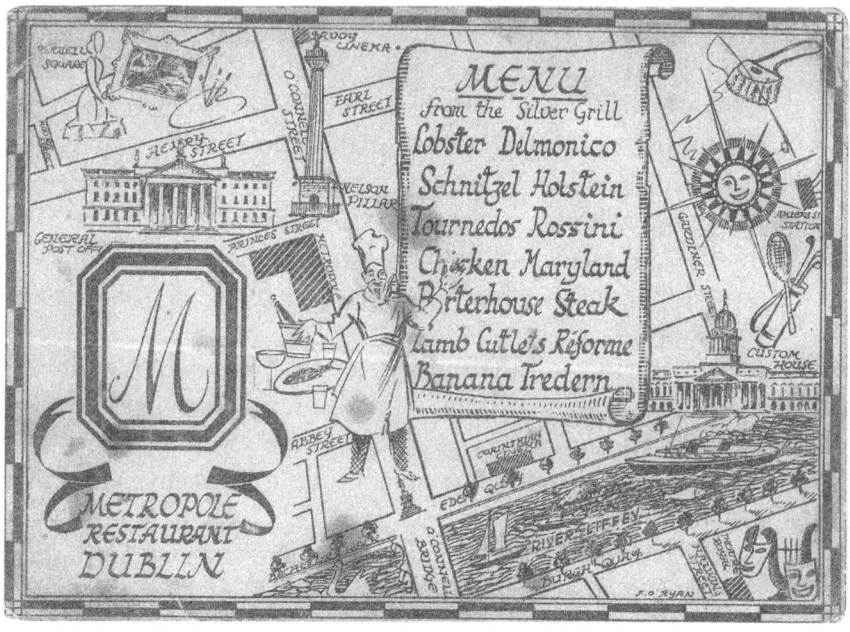

A postcard menu (circa 1950) from the Metropole, Dublin

Pate Brisee
(Unsweetened basic pie crust pastry)

Most everyone at one time or another has made pastry for pies, flans, tarts, tartlettes, or quiche, and there are probably dozens of variations for the recipe.

You may nonchalantly think, "This is simple, I'll just throw these ingredients together..." not so! Making pate brisee is not to be treated lightly; there are certain rules which MUST be followed in order for it to be successful. If they are not, then your efforts will be worthless.

My explanation of the reasons for following the instructions will aid you in understanding the difference between success and failure, and prevent you from committing mistakes when preparing the perfect and delicious pate brisee.

Some pastry recipes use shortening or lard exclusively. However, I prefer to mostly use pure, creamery, unsalted butter for its rich taste, also, it is less artery-clogging than shortening or lard. The following recipe for pate brisee is one I have developed through experimenting with ingredient quantities for many years.

A good rule of thumb is to assemble all the ingredients beforehand, and when ready to prepare the pastry, don't linger or waste time; work rapidly in order to keep the ingredients as cold as possible.

Pate Brisee (For Pies, Flans, Tarts, Tartlettes)

• • • • • • • • • •

(Makes one 12-inch tart or pie, approximately 22 ounces of pastry)

INGREDIENTS

2½ cups (11 ½ oz) unbleached all-purpose flour (or pastry flour if available)
1½ sticks (6 oz) cold, unsalted butter
4 tablespoons (2 oz) Crisco butter-flavored vegetable shortening
½ teaspoon salt
6 tablespoons (3 fl. ozs) iced spring-water
1 tablespoon fresh lemon juice, or, 1 tablespoon of white vinegar
1 medium egg yolk
(If a sweet pastry (Pate Sucree) is required, add 6 tablespoons (3 oz) sugar)

• • • • • • • • • •

METHOD:
1. The very first thing to do is place a large glass of iced spring-water in the refrigerator.
2. Refrigerate the butter and shortening till chilled. Then remove and cut into small cubes.
3. Sieve the flour and salt together, holding the sieve up high to give it a good airing.
4. In a large bowl, add the chilled butter to the dry ingredients, and with your **fingertips** (the coolest part of your hand), crumble the mixture into small, pea-sized pieces. Human hands normally maintain a body temperature of 98.6 degrees F. (37 degrees C) which is much too warm for making pastry (hence the use of fingertips only); the less human touch the better. Using a hand-held pastry cutter or a food processor is a good substitute, just be careful not to over-pulse the dry ingredients in the processor.
5. Add the butter-flavored vegetable shortening and crumble it into the mixture in pea-sized pieces.
6. In a small bowl, whisk the egg yolk, one tablespoon lemon juice, and the six tablespoons of the pre-refrigerated iced spring-water together and pour it into the dry mixture, and using a table dinner-

fork, form the mixture into a ball. It is very important to pause and allow the mixture to rest for 10 seconds after the addition of the liquid ingredients in order to allow the flour to absorb them.

In the event the mixture is still too dry, you may add one or possibly two teaspoons of the iced spring-water, but only if it is absolutely necessary, because in order to keep the pastry short, it is critical not to over-add water. If you add too much water, it will create too much gluten, and an excessive water-gluten formation will make the pastry tough.

The amount of water can never be exact, as the exact amount varies depending on the consistency of the flour and butter used.

7. Because alcohol does not provide for the creation of gluten, you may substitute half the iced spring-water with an equal amount of unflavored vodka. The vodka is 40 percent alcohol by volume, and it evaporates as much as 50 percent during the baking process, and leaves no alcohol flavor after evaporation.

8. If overly concerned about cholesterol intake, omit the egg yolk. The pastry will still be tender.

9. Very lightly, quickly knead the pastry dough three times with both hands, preferably on a lightly floured, pre-refrigerated, cold marble slab (do not over-work it), and bring it all together into a flat square block or round disc. Wrap the pastry tightly in plastic food-wrap film, and refrigerate and rest it for one hour before use. Resting the pastry is imperative as it relaxes the gluten, resulting in a more tender, crumbly pastry.

10. Pate brisee may be made ahead, double-wrapped tightly, first in greaseproof paper, and second in plastic food-wrap film in order to protect it from freezer-burn. Mark with the date on the outside of the wrapper, and frozen for up to one month.

• • • • • • • • • •

One of the most objectionable faults about baking pastry is producing a pie or tart with a soggy bottom. In an effort to avoid that, I recommend the following tips:

•   To achieve the best baking results, place a pizza stone, or four eight-inch-by-eight-inch, (or smaller), unglazed clay tiles on the middle rack of the oven, and place the pie, flan, tart, tartlette, or quiche on them to bake. Unglazed clay tiles may be purchased at most hardware stores.

- When baking pies, tarts, or quiche, use Pyrex (tempered glass) or a clay pan with a strong glaze or a perforated heavy metal pie-pan. They are all good conductors of heat.
- I myself have two 11-inch round, fluted removable-bottom pie pans that I have perforated by drilling 25 holes in them with a half-inch drill bit. This allows steam (if any) to escape.
- I also use a 16-inch round perforated pizza tray for baking a traditional french apple tart.
- Pies, flans, tarts, tartlettes, and quiche should be baked at 375 degrees F. (190.5 C), Gas Mark 5, until golden brown, and depending on the filling, calibration of the oven, and size of the item, may take from 30 to 45 minutes.
- Use ceramic or dried beans on foil if baking blind, and if baking blind, refrigerate the pastry shell in its pan for 30 minutes, then freeze it for 20 minutes before immediately baking it until golden brown at 375 degrees F. (190.5 C), Gas Mark 5.
- Fruit pie bottoms will be less soggy when covered with cake crumbs or rolled oats before the cool, wet filling is applied.
- Always allow a pastry pie to sit and cool for at least two hours in order for it to set before cutting and serving.
- Use raw sugar on top of brushed-on egg white on the pie 15 minutes prior to finishing baking (the sugar won't break down).
- Unsalted butter is best for making pastry because it has less milk solids, salt, and water content than salted sweet butter, and therefore does not alter the recipe, resulting in a flakier pastry. Also it allows cakes to rise higher, and makes cookies crispier.
- Butter-flavored vegetable shortening, lard, and egg yolk tenderize pastry dough.
- Unbleached all-purpose flour produces strong and firm pastry.
- Purchase a marble slab small enough to fit in your refrigerator and store it there until needed for use in rolling-out pastry.
- Pastry making requires a certain amount of practice before you become perfect. Do not become discouraged if you are not successful with your first or second attempt; remember, practice makes perfect.

Genoese Gateaux, Torte, and Wedding Cakes

- All ovens are not always thermostatically calibrated alike; consequently, oven temperatures do vary, especially convection ovens (fan-assisted). Careful testing of one's oven should always be performed in order to learn the oven's capabilities and faults.
- Cakes should be baked at 300 degrees Fahrenheit (148.8 degrees Celsius) to 325 degrees F. (162.7 degrees C). Larger, thicker cakes require a longer time period than thin layers.
- Flour differs in weight and quality in every country in the world.
- Free circulation of oven heat is essential to successful baking.
- When baking cakes in Pyrex glass pans, reduce the oven temperature by 25 degrees F. (14 degrees C).
- When baking an upside-down cake, line the pan with aluminum foil before filling it.
- Cake and pie pans should be placed in the center of the oven and not touch each other or the walls of the oven.
- Cakes will stay moist longer when kept wrapped in a damp cloth.
- To cut cleanly through a lemon meringue pie, or any cake, use a knife dipped in hot water after each slice.
- When a chocolate cake recipe calls for flouring the baking pan, use cocoa powder.
- When slicing a cake horizontally for filling, using a slicing knife is better than a serrated knife. A serrated knife creates crumbs.
- Cake tins should be made of the best quality metal.
- Egg yolks increase the tenderness of cakes.
- All ingredients for cake making should be at room temperature.
- Yeast dough rises faster with sugar added to the yeast sponge.

- Royal icings will become softer when glycerin is added after beating.
- Icings dry quickly and with a high shine when placed in a warm oven for a few minutes.
- At altitudes above 3,000 feet, lower air pressure affects cake-baking times. Always refer to local guidelines.
- One of the most popular cakes in Europe is the gateaux, or torte. They can be adapted for any occasion such as birthdays, engagements, weddings, anniversaries, christenings, Mothers Day, graduations, confirmations, Bar (or Bas) Mitzvahs, congratulations, Christmas, Easter, arts, sports, welcome home, bon voyage, Halloween, and indeed divorce (or other special festive occasions).
- I am of the opinion that the world's most famous cake is the Austrian Viennese Sacher Torte, a very rich chocolate layer cake, named after the Hotel Sacher in Vienna, where it was created. The original recipe is still a closely guarded secret.
- As a former Chef Patissier, I have prepared the four most popular and important wedding cakes in the western world. I urge all apprentice chefs to study and eventually learn how to prepare them. They are:
  1. English-Irish dried heavy fruit wedding cake.
  2. French Profiterole Croquembouche (crunch in the mouth) wedding cake.
  3. Italian Traditional 3–7 layer Torte Nuziali (wedding cake).
  4. American Madeira wedding cake.

Pate Brisee, Chocolate & Berry Bateau

Buche de Nóel

Chocolate Carrack (Curls) Gateaux

Croquembouche

American Wedding Cake

Weights and Measures

Naturally, I did not scientifically create the measurement tables contained in this text; they were carefully established by scientists long before I was born.

I did, however, take several measurement tables I had collected as a teenage culinary student and combined and expanded them, resulting in what I consider to be the most detailed and comprehensive measurement tables I have seen in any publication to date.

Because of the fractionally minute differences between American Standard and metric measurements, it is impossible to be exact; nevertheless, these tables are accurate enough to ensure the practitioner successful results should you intermingle measurements within a recipe (although I do not recommend doing so).

Hopefully, my adaptation of these conversion charts will take some of the guess work out of your culinary endeavors.

Most American recipe ingredients are given in measures, rather than in weight, although some larger recipes are given in weight.

Only three countries in the world still use the U.S. Standard system of measurement: U.S.A., Liberia (in Africa), Myanmar (formerly Burma).

All others use the metric system.

The metric (metre) system of weights and measures was created in France by Antoine Laurant de Lavoisier (1743– 1794), who was known as the father of modern chemistry. His theory, established in 1801, is that the metre is one ten-millionth part of a quadrant of the Earth through Paris.

The liter (litre) is the volume of a cube of one-tenth metre side.

The gram (gramme) is one-thousandth of the weight of a litre of water at four degrees Centigrade, (39.2 degrees Fahrenheit).

Metric measurements are: meters (metre) for length, grams (gramme) for weight, liters (litre) for volume.

To convert a Fahrenheit temperature to Centigrade, do the following:

a. Subtract 32
b. Multiply by 5
c. Divide by 9

To convert a Centrigrade temperature to Fahrenheit, do the following:

a. Multiply by 9
b. Divide by 5
c. Add 32

Conversion Tables for
Mass & Weight Measures

All measuring devices should be the official exact pre-measured type, not spoons or cups used at the table as these would be inaccurate. All measures should be level, and depending on the ingredient, *will vary in weight*. Keep in mind, some ingredients are *lighter* or *heavier* than others; for example, cups of rice, sugar, couscous, or flour do NOT weigh equally. Therefore, the mathematical conversion guides that follow in this section will be immensely helpful to you. The size of the first smaller measurement is open to interpretation.

American Standard	Metric
One Pinch or Dash = ...	1/16 teaspoon
0.0353 oz = ...	1 gram
.25 oz = ¼ oz = ...	7.087 grams
3 teas = ½ oz = 1 tbls = ...	14.17grams
2 tbls = 1 oz = 1/8 cup = ...	28.34 grams
3 tbls = 1½oz = ...	45.52grams
4 tbls = 2oz = ¼cup = ...	56.69 grams
5–1/3 tbls = 2½ oz = 1/3 cup = ...	70.87 grams
6 tbls = 3oz = ...	85.04 grams
7 tbls = 3½ oz. = 3/8cup + 1 tbls = ...	100 grams
8 tbls = 4oz = ½cup = ¼1b = ...	113.39 grams
9 tbls = 4 ½ oz = ...	127.57 grams
10 tbls = 5 oz = ...	141.74 grams

12 tbls = 6 oz = ¾ cup = ...170.09 grams
14 tbls = 7 oz = ...198.44 grams
16 tbls = 8 oz = 1 cup = ½1b = ...226.79grams
18 tbls = 9 oz = ...255.14 grams
20 tbls = 10 oz = 1 ¼ cups = ...283.49 grams
22 tbls = 11 oz = .311.84 grams
24 tbls = 12 oz = 1 ½cups = ¾ 1b = ...340.19 grams
26 tbls = 13 oz = .368.54 grams
28 tbls = 14 oz = 1 ¾ cups = ...396.89 grams
30 tbls = 15 oz = .425.24 grams
32 tbls = 16 oz = 2 cups = 1 lb = ...453.59 grams
34 tbls = 17 oz = .481.94 grams
36 tbls = 18 oz = 2 ¼ cups = ...510.29 grams
38 tbls = 19 oz = .538.64 grams
40 tbls = 20 oz = 2 ½ cups = 1 ¼ lb = ...566.99 grams
48 tbls = 24 oz = 3 cups = 1½ lb = ...680.38 grams
64 tbls = 32 oz = 4 cups = 2 lb = ...907.18 grams

• • • • • • • • • •

35.3 oz = 4.4 cups = 2.21 lb = 1,000 grams = 1 kilogram
5 lbs. = 2.26 kilograms
10 lbs. = 4.53 kilograms
15 lbs. = 6.80 kilograms
20 lbs. = 9.07 kilograms
25 lbs. = 11.33 kilograms
50 lbs. = 22.67 kilograms
100 lbs. = 45.30 kilograms
.98421 long ton or 1.1023 English or short ton =1 Metric ton

Conversion Tables for Liquid Measures

All measuring devices should be the official exact, pre-measured type, not spoons or cups used at the table, as these would be inaccurate. All measures should be level spoons, ounces, cups, milliliters, and liters.

To convert ounces to cups, divide the number of ounces by eight.

The sizes of the first two smaller measurements are open to interpretation.

American Standard   Metric

Dash = ...1/16 teas
.033814 fl oz = 1/8 teas = ...1 milliliter (ml)
60 drops = 1 teas = ...5 ml
3 teas = 1 tbls = ½floz . . . . .15 ml
2 tbls = 1 fl oz = 1/8cup = ...29.573ml
3 tbls = 1 ½ fl oz = ...44.34 ml
4 tbls = 2 fl.oz. = ¼ cup = ...59.14ml
5 tbls + 1 teas= 2½ fl oz = 1/3cup =. 78.83ml
6 tbls = 3 fl oz = ...88.71 ml
7 tbls - 3 ½ fl oz = ...103.46 ml
8 tbls = 4fl oz = ½ cup = ¼ pint = 1 gill =... . . . . . .118.28 ml
9 tbls = 4½fl oz = ...133.06 ml
10 tbls = 5 fl oz = 2/3 cups = ...147.85 ml
12 tbls = 6 fl oz = ¾ cup = ...177.42 ml
16 tbls = 8fl oz = 1 cup = ½ pint = 2 gills = ...236.56 ml
24 tbls = 12 fl oz = 1&1/2 cups = ¾ pint = ...354.84 ml

32 tbls = 16 fl oz = 2 cups = 1 pint = 4 gills = ...473.12 ml
34 tbls = 17 fl oz = 1 pt & 1 fl oz = ...500 ml
48 tbls = 24 fl oz = 3 cups = 1 ½ pints = ...709.68 ml
64 tbls = 32 fl oz = 4 cups = 2 pints = 1 quart = . . .946.24 ml
34 fl oz = 4 ¼ cups = 1 qt+2 oz = ...1 litre
64 fl oz = 8 cups = 4 pints = 2 quarts = ½ gallon = .1.895 liters
16 cups = 8pints = 4 quarts = 1 gallon = ...3.79 liters
16 pints = 8 quarts = 2 gallons = ...7.58 liters
64 pints = 32 quarts = 8 gallons = ...30.32 liters

Britain and other foreign countries use weights such as Avoirdupois, which is the foreign system of weights for all commodities except gold, silver, platinum, gems, and pharmaceutical drugs (Troy weight) based on the following units.

Avoirdupois (French) "Avoir"= to have. "Du"= some. "Pois"= weight.
　27&11/32 grains = 1 dram
　437.5 grains = 16 drams = 1 oz
　7,000 grains = 16 oz = 1 lb
　14lbs = 1 stone
　28lbs = 2 stone = 1 quarter
　100lbs = 1 short hundredweight (cwt), or Cental
　112lbs = 4 quarters = 1 hundredweight (cwt)
　2,000lbs = 1 short ton
　2,240 lbs = 20 hundredweight = 1 long (or gross) ton

Troy (Precious Metals- Gold, Silver, Platinum, Gems, Pharmaceutical Drugs).
　24 grains = 1 pennyweight (dwt)
　480 grains = 20 pennyweights = 1 oz (also the Apothecaries ounce, 480 Avoirdupois grains)

Volume Metric Conversion Guide

When You Know	Multiply by	To find
Milliliters	0.20	Teaspoons
Milliliters	0.06	Tablespoons
Milliliters	0.034	Fluid ounces
Liters	4.23	Cups
Liters	2.12	Pints
Liters	1.06	Quarts
Liters	0.26	Gallons
Teaspoons	4.93	Milliliters
Tablespoons	14.78	Milliliters
Fluid ounces	29.57	Milliliters
Cups	0.24	Liters
Pints	0.47	Liters
Quarts	0.95	Liters
Gallons	3.79	Liters

Mass & Weight Conversion Guide

When you know	Multiply by	To find
Groins	64.79891	Milligrams
Grains	0.064799	Grams
Ounces	28.349523	Grams
Grams	0.035	Ounces
Ounces	0.0283495	Kilograms
Pounds	0.4535924	Kilograms
Stones	6.3502932	Kilograms
Hundredweights	50.802345	Kilograms
Tons	1016.0469	Kilograms
Kilograms	2.21	Pounds
Tons	1.01605	Metric tonnes
Tons	1.10	Short tons
Short Tons (2,000 lb)	0.91	Tons

Oven Temperature Conversions

Fahrenheit . . . . .Celsius . . . . .Gas Mark

Very Low 250 . . . . .120 .1/2
Low 275 . . . . .140 .1
Very Slow 300 . . . . .150 .2
Slow 325 . . . . .170 .3
Moderate 350 . . . . .180 .4
Moderate 375 . . . . .190 .5
Moderately Hot 400 . . . . .200 .6
Fairly Hot 425 . . . . .220 .7
Hot 450 . . . . .230 .8
Very Hot 475 . . . . .240 .9
Very, Very Hot 500 . . . . .260 .10

Roasting Temperatures

Temperature degrees are approximations.

Beef (Not touching the bone)
Rare 130 degrees F. (54 C.)
Medium 160 degrees F. (71C.)
Well-Done 180 degrees F. (82 C.)

Lamb (Not touching the bone)
Pink 140 degrees F. (60 C.)
Medium-Rare 145 Degrees F. (63 C.)
Well-Done 165 degrees F. (74 C.)

Pork & Veal (Not touching the bone)
160 degrees F. (71 C.)

Poultry
Chicken Breast 170 degrees F. (77 C.)
Chicken Thigh 185 degrees F. (85 C.)
Duck Thigh 180 degrees F. (82 C.)
Turkey Breast 170 degrees F. (77 C)
Turkey Thigh 180 degrees F. (82.2 C)

Ice Cream

Ice cream is a frozen dessert usually made from dairy products such as fresh milk, real cream, eggs, pure sugar, fruits, nuts, chocolate, and other all-natural ingredients and flavorings.

The secret to making creamy ice-cream is to slowly incorporate air into the chosen ingredients while preventing large ice crystals from forming. That air content may be as high as 50 per cent.

Most varieties contain natural sugar (sucrose), although some are made with other sweeteners like honey and artificial sweeteners, flavorings and colorings.

Some average, inexpensive grocery store brands have been known by the U.S. Food and Drug Administration to contain synthetic additives, which can be poisonous, and laboratory analyses have shown the following:

1. Diethylene Glucol (DEG) - Used as an egg substitute in ice creams. Also a glycerin-contaminated poison used in anti-freeze and paint removers.
2. Piperonal - Vanilla substitute. Another use is anti-head- lice medicine.
3. Aldehyde C17 - Gives you cherry taste in ice creams. Used in dyes, plastic, and rubber factories.
4. Ethyl Acetate - Pineapple substitute in pineapple ice creams. Known to find uses in leather and textiles. Causes lung, liver, and heart damage.
5. Butraldehyde - Provides nut flavor in ice creams. Used in rubber cement.

6. Amyl Acetate - Banana flavor. Good oil paint solvent.

7. Benzyl acetate - Tasty strawberry flavor and a good nitrate solvent.

So, if you buy inexpensive grocery store brand ice creams, READ THE INGREDIENTS!

My advice is if you don't know and understand the names of all the ingredients...don't buy it! There are some ice creams available for those who are gluten and lactose intolerant, or allergic to dairy, protein, or are vegan.

Ice - Cream Headache (Brain freeze): The rapid constriction and swelling of the trigeminal nerve in the palate (roof of the mouth) to the brain from the quick consumption of cold ice cream, ice-pops, beverages, and foods.

Pressing the tongue against the roof of the mouth to warm the area, or tilting the head back for about 10 seconds are the only known remedies.

Edible Flowers

Do not use edible flowers from a florist, nursery, garden store, or those found growing on the side of the road (or those that grow near lawns that are chemically treated with weed killer) as edible garnishes, unless they are labeled as organically grown, as they may have been sprayed with pesticides or herbicides.

You should use only those you have grown yourself from seed, so you can be certain about how they have been treated.

It is best to hand-water rather than mechanically irrigate edible flowers, as mechanical irrigation may lead to disease.

It is also best to pick them just before using, as they have a short shelf life, although you can refrigerate them in plastic bags for a short period.

Many edible flowers are believed to be medicinal, used to slow and regulate heart palpitations, and some contain vitamins A & C and minerals.

Edible flower petals can be crystallized by lightly brushing them with lightly beaten egg-white, a sprinkling of superfine sugar, and allowing them to dry. In the event you are cautious about the raw egg white, you may substitute it with one tablespoon of Gum Arabic and one tablespoon of water.

When the petals are completely dry, store them in an airtight non-plastic container. They should be used within three to four months.

Persons who suffer from hay-fever, asthma, or allergies should NOT eat edible flowers.

Sampling of Edible Flowers

• • • • • • • • • • •

* Elderberry * Calendula * Dianthus * Primrose * Wild Geranium *
Roses * Honeysuckle * Hollyhocks * Daisy (Bellis perennis) * Johnny-
jump-up * Red clover * Mallow * Yarrow * Tulip * Bee balm * Borage *
Carnations * Fennel * Mint * Forget-me-nots * Gladioluses * Nastur-
tiums * Pansies * Spring crocus * Baby's breath * California poppy * Vi-
olets * Forsythia * Dogwood * Dandelion * Phlox * Petunia * Peony *
Gardenia * Marigolds * Impatiens * Hibiscus * Snapdragons * Yucca *
Day lilies * Squash * Flowering herbs * Lilac * Arugula * Basil * Begonia
* Chives * Dill * Geraniums *Lavender * Lemon Verbena * Passion-
flower * Rosemary * Safflower * Sage * Society Garlic * Sunflower *
Zucchini

Food and Wine Accompaniments

Hors d'oeuvre . . . . .White Bordeaux, white burgundy, Loire, Cotes du Rhone, Beaujolais Maconnais, Alsace.

Oysters . . . . .Any dry white wine, extra dry champagne, stout.

Soup . . . . .Dry sherry

Fish . . . . .Any dry white wine, extra dry champagne

Light Meat or Chicken . . . . . .Dry white wine, dry Champagne

Red Meat or Game . . . . .Red burgundy, Red Bordeaux (Claret)

Dessert . . . . .Any sweet white wine, sparkling wine, demi-Sec champagne

Cheese . . . . .Any red or white wine, port, dry sherry, dry Marsala, Alsace, sweet or dry champagne

- Champagne can be served throughout dinner.
- Do not serve red wine with fish (except salmon)
- Do not serve a sweet wine before a dry wine
- Do not serve a heavy wine before a light wine
- Do not drink any spirits (such as whiskey etc) with oysters
- All white wines and champagne should be served COOLED, not chilled
- All red wines should be served at room temperature
- Wine freezes at 20 degrees Fahrenheit. (Minus 7 degrees Celsius)
- Alcohol Boils at 173 degrees Fahrenheit. (78 degrees Celsius)

- Vinegar freezes at 28 degrees Fahrenheit. (Minus 2.5 degrees Celsius)
- Red wine can cook awhile in sauces
- White wine CANNOT cook; it is light bodied and will break down. Add it to sauces last.
- Wine connoisseurs aerate or oxygenate wine into a glass or carafe in order to allow it to breathe properly which results in better bouquet and flavor.

Genetically Modified Food
(G.M. foods or Biotech foods)

Genetically modified food is probably the most controversial, complicated, and complex subject in the history of food processing.

The scientific data available is so enormous, and public opinion for and against G.M.F.'s so strong, I have decided to simply provide just a miniscule amount of data and allow readers to further research and decide for themselves which viewpoint to adopt.

Genetically modified foods were first introduced into the marketplace in 1996. Scientists first discovered DNA is transferable between organisms in 1946; the first genetically modified plant was produced in 1983; in 1994 the tomato was genetically modified for human consumption. Soybeans and potatoes followed suit in 1995, canola in 1996, alfalfa in 2005, and as of 2011, the U.S. leads all other countries with as high as 93 per cent of G.M.F.'s in some foods, and 70 per cent of all processed foods contained a G.M.F. ingredient.

The U.S. Food and Drug Administration (USFDA), the U.S. Department of Agriculture (USDA), and the U.S. Environmental Protection Agency (USEPA) regulate the production and safety of genetically modified food, but do not require the labeling of G.M.F.'s as do the European Union, Japan, Malaysia, and Australia.

As recently as December 2012, the USFDA published a 158-page environmental assessment report that found genetically engineered Atlantic salmon was safe to eat, and also would not hurt the environment. Angry opponents of the move commonly refer to the AquAdvantage salmon as a "Frankenfish."

AquAdvantage salmon grows twice as fast as conventional salmon because a growth hormone gene derived from the Chinook variety of salmon has been spliced into its DNA.

In the event this process is approved by the USFDA and USEPA, it will be the first genetically modified animal for food use to pass that milestone in the United States.

In comparison to the U.S., the European approach to G.M.F.'s is one of trepidation, with protesters destroying trial crops, claiming natural and organic solutions to reduce chemical use is the answer, and not G.M.F.'s, and critics have objected to G.M. foods on several grounds, including safety, economic, and ecological issues and concerns.

Whether one is for or against G.M.F.'s, a 2008 review published by the Royal Society of Medicine stated that G.M.F.'s have been eaten by millions of people worldwide for over 15 years, with no reports of ill effects.

My personal, specific advice is to seek medical, legal, financial, and risk management advice on the subject from a licensed professional knowledgeable in that area.

Food Allergies and Intolerances

Food allergies and food intolerances are not the same thing.

A food allergy such as Casein occurs when your body's immune system mistakenly thinks the protein is harmful and triggers the immune system to release chemicals, or antibodies such as histamine into the bloodstream for protection, which cause symptoms that may include: difficulty breathing, swelling of lips, mouth, tongue, face and throat, unconsciousness, nasal congestion, sneezing, runny nose, coughing, wheezing, itchy eyes, skin hives, rash, or red itchy skin. The most common food items that cause allergic reactions are: milk, eggs, peanuts, tree nuts, fish, shellfish, wheat, and soy.

Most people with these allergies develop them when they are infants and outgrow them as they get older. However, some people do not outgrow them and continue to be allergic as adults, and other adults may become allergic to foods they once ate with no problem. However it is unusual to develop an allergy to milk proteins later in life, although it can happen.

A potentially deadly reaction to an allergen is called anaphylaxis.

People with asthma and a casein allergy are at greater risk of having an anaphylactic reaction to food. Therefore, avoidance of all foods that contain milk or milk products is the best prevention, as even miniscule amounts of casein may be enough to trigger a life-threatening reaction.

Casein is a protein called Phosphoprotein in milk.

Lactose intolerance, a symptom of gluten intolerance, is a condition whereby your body is unable to digest lactose, a form of sugar (glucose and galactose) commonly found in milk. Lactose intolerance is not preventable; eliminating all dairy products such as ice cream, yogurt, cheese, and butter from one's diet is the only prevention.

Symptoms of lactose intolerance are: gas, flatulence, bloating, cramps, and diarrhea.

Studies have estimated that 98 per cent of Asian Americans, 75 per cent of African Americans, and 25 per cent of Caucasian Americans suffer from Lactose Intolerance.

"Lactose Free" foods may still contain casein; one should always read labels in order to be completely safe.

Melon, bananas, cucumber, tomatoes, celery, and peaches can also aggravate certain pollen and grass allergies.

The safest animal foods for lactose intolerant sufferers are grass-fed beef, free-range chicken, and New Zealand lamb and other New Zealand grass-fed animal foods.

Another milk protein associated with allergies is whey.

Whey is the liquid material created as a by-product of cheese production, and some people are allergic to both casein and whey. An over-the-counter antihistamine or epinephrine shot is the best known remedy.

rBST: (Recombinant bovine somatotropin), also known as rBGH (Recombinant bovine growth hormone), is a genetically engineered drug injected into dairy cows to induce them to increase milk production, typically by five to 15 per cent. It is estimated that 15 to 20 per cent of the cows in the U.S. are injected with this hormone. It was approved by the F.D.A. in 1993.

When rBST is injected into a cow, it elevates levels of another powerful growth hormone called IGF-1. In excessive amounts it has been linked in hundreds of studies to an increase in breast, prostate, colon, lung, and other cancers in humans.

Food intolerances, or non-allergic food hypersensitivities, do not involve the immune system, and are not true food allergies. Intolerance is a physiological response associated with a particular food or compound found in various foods; it is sometimes a delayed negative reaction to a food, beverage, food additive, or compound that produces symptoms in one or more body organs and systems.

A food intolerance does not require the presence of antibodies in one's system. Rather, this can be the result of one's body's ability to absorb nutrients.

It's symptoms tend to appear gradually, and are usually less serious, and are limited to problems with digestion.

Gluten – Gluten Allergy –
Gluten Intolerance (Celiac Disease)

Gluten is a composite of the proteins gliadin and glutenin.

It is an elastic, sticky, gluey substance found in wheat, sprouted wheat, white and wheat flours including: all-purpose, cake, bread, pastry, wholemeal, wheatmeal, wheatgerm, graham, enriched and unbleached flours, wheat berries, high protein or high gluten flours, bran, Semolina, bulgar, durum, einkorn, farina, farro, crossbred hybrids, couscous, rye, barley, oat (other than gluten-free). It is also found in triticale, most cereals, acker meal, food starch, pasta, ice cream, dextrin (containing wheat), some soup bases, spelt, kamut, soy sauce, Worcestershire powder (which contains barley and malt) in some salad dressings and is not gluten-free, marinades that contain gluten, (gluten-free is available), surimi (mock crab meat), ales, beer, hot dogs, processed meats, and seasonings such as Monosodium Glutamate (MSG), which is a Japanese sodium salt of glutamic acid from seaweed. MSG is a natural amino acid and flavor enhancer of balanced foods. Some people suffer palpitations and other reactions from ingesting MSG.

U.S. Food and Drug Administration approved gluten-free flours are: Quinoa flour, almond flour, soy flour, bean flours, coconut flour, buckwheat flour, chickpea flour, amaranth flour, millet flour, brown rice flour, oat flour, ground flaxseed flour, potato starch flour and corn flour.

Gluten helps dough rise and gives baked goods structure and texture.

Gluten allergy is an abnormal or hypersensitive human response or reaction to specific foods containing the tiniest amount of gluten.

Reaction symptoms range from stomach upset to asthma-like attacks, which can be very serious.

Gluten intolerance, also known as Celiac Disease, is an inability of the human body to absorb or endure the substance gluten and proteins, fats, nutrients, carbohydrates, and vitamins and minerals, which are all necessary for good health.

Celiac Disease is a digestive medical condition triggered by eating the protein gluten, causing damage to the absorptive surface of the small intestine.

Reaction symptoms are diarrhea, vomiting, bloating, fatigue, eczema, dehydration, and abdominal distention.

An estimated three million persons in the U.S. have an intolerance to gluten and are affected by Celiac Disease (CD), and the U.S. Food and Drug Administration recently requires all foods labeled "gluten-free", "no gluten", "free of gluten", and "without gluten" must contain less than 20 parts per million of gluten.

If Celiac Disease is not diagnosed and treated it can lead to many diseases down the road such as nutritional deficiencies, infertility, miscarriages, delayed or stunted growth, cancer, fibromyalgia, type 1 diabetes, osteoporosis, and rheumatoid arthritis, among other conditions.

The only treatment for Celiac Disease is a diet without gluten, and a gluten-free diet will not necessarily help you lose weight, and one should not even think about it without consulting a doctor.

Individuals who suffer from these three different entities must avoid contact with gluten, and remove gluten-inclusive recipes from their daily lives at all costs.

Celiac sufferers should have their own separate cooking utensils, silverware, plate-ware and napkins, as even a trace amount of gluten can make someone who suffers from CD sick.

When eating out in restaurants, CD sufferers are not just being fussy about their food, they have legitimate health concerns, and restaurant management, professional chefs, cooks, and servers, really need to understand the seriousness of gluten intolerance, Celiac Disease, and gluten/wheat allergy in general.

It seems CD sufferers are increasing in numbers, therefore gluten-free demand has been overwhelming. It is estimated that the U.S. demand for gluten-free products is so robust it represents more than 4 billion dollars in annual sales. Now I ask you, "who wouldn't want a part of that market?" Consequently, restaurants would be business-smart to have designated staff and separate preparation areas and equipment in order to make every effort to properly cater to them so that they may earn their trust and convert them into regular customers. Churches certainly do, as many now offer gluten-free communion wafers upon request.

Garnishes

- Parsley and watercress sprigs
- Crystallized ginger
- Sprigs of fresh herbs
- Edible fresh flowers
- Grapefruit baskets
- Fleurons (puff pastry crescents)
- Two-inch scallions, chives, leeks, scored julienne each end and iced
- Radish flowers
- Sprigs of black, red, green grapes
- Sieved hard-boiled egg
- Snow-pea flower
- Baby spring carrots with greenery
- Filled cucumber boats
- Filled baby beets with horseradish cream
- Carpaccio of cantaloupe
- Smoked salmon or tomato rose, cucumber rind leaf
- Hard-boiled egg white flower with black caviar
- Emptied orange shell filled with port wine Jello in wedges
- Artichoke bottom with peas and black caviar
- Apple bird
- Deep fried, julienne white leeks
- Deep fried Brussels sprout leaves
- Deep fried zucchini blossoms
- Deep fried baby spinach leaves
- Deep fried parsley sprigs
- Sautéed grape or cherry tomatoes

- Chicory leaves with berries
- Pomegranate arils
- Pickled ginger root
- Julienne black truffles
- Sliced star fruit
- Bamboo or pineapple leaves
- Red beet julienne
- Sugar coated herb leaves and stems
- Vanilla beans
- Pesto/miso dots surrounding an entrée
- Mushroom caps with duxelles
- Broiled fresh fig halves
- Red leaf radicchio leaves
- Coconut shells with fresh fruit
- Deep fried potato rose on a toothpick
- Lemon twists and flowers

Mercury in Fish

Health authorities encourage people to eat more fish, not less, because its highly nutritious, can improve cardiac health, and provides benefits to a developing fetus.

Mercury, a metallic element discharged by coal-fired power plants, can build up in the human body over years, causing neurological problems, including memory loss and personality disorders. It presents the greatest danger to children, pregnant women, and women who plan to become pregnant because it can damage the neurological nervous system of the developing child.

Fish with the highest mercury levels are large predators, such as sharks, swordfish, mackerel, and largemouth bass, which contain in their flesh all the mercury from the fish they've eaten. Fish bought at stores generally present less of a problem than fish from a mercury hot spot, so long as you don't overdo consumption.

But even with store-bought fish, there has been extensive debate among the Food and Drug Administration, Environmental Protection Agency and environmental groups about the mercury risks versus the health benefits of seafood.

Childbearing-age women and small children should never eat shark, and no one should eat shark that is 43 inches or longer.

Minerals – Proteins – Carbohydrates – Vitamins

Minerals:
Minerals are essential to all life, including plants and organisms.

There are 10 or more minerals known to be present in foods.

The six most important minerals are calcium, phosphorus, iron, potassium, iodine, and sodium.

Calcium: milk, cheese, and other milk products, greens, salmon, sardines with bones.

Phosphorus: poultry, fish, meats, cereals, nuts, legumes, milk and milk products.

Iron: marine fish, shellfish, seaweed, iodized salt.

Potassium: dried herbs, avocados, paprika or red chili powder, cocoa powder, chocolate, dried apricots, prunes, currants, raisins, pistachios and other nuts, pumpkin, squash, sunflower and flax seeds, pompano, salmon, halibut, tuna, white beans, dates.

Iodine: ocean fish, shellfish, sea vegetables, cranberries, asparagus, carrots, tomatoes, rhubarb, potatoes, peas, strawberries, mushrooms, egg yolk, soybeans.

Sodium: (sodium chloride or table salt) A silver-white metallic element, the base of soda.

Healthy adults should consume no more than one teaspoon -2,000 mg of sodium per day.

Processed foods are the biggest culprits containing sodium.

Proteins:

Proteins are composed of amino acids, and there are 28 of these commonly found in foods, eight being essential to adults and 10 to growing children.

These essential amino acids can only be supplied by the foods we eat, and animal protein usually contains all of them.

Vegetable proteins are normally deficient in some essential amino acids, but if animal foods are excluded from the diet, carefully combining protein from different vegetable sources, such as grains, nuts and legumes, will ensure an adequate protein intake.

Carbohydrates:

There are three types of carbohydrates.

Sugar: sugar, honey, jam, syrup, dried fruit, fresh fruit, (especially bananas).

Starches: flour, cereals, bread, pasta, rice, potatoes, starchy vegetables.

Cellulose: unrefined cereals and nuts, dietary fiber, wholemeal bread.

Vitamins:

Vitamins are organic substances widely distributed in natural foodstuffs. They are believed to be necessary to certain vital functions of the human body.

So far, nearly 20 vitamins have been discovered, of which the following four are considered the most important in food.

Vitamin A: Found in butter, margarine, cheese, eggs, herrings, sardines, liver, almonds, peanuts, carrots, greens, sweet potatoes, beet greens, winter squash, cantaloupe, broccoli, dried apricots, whole milk and cream.

Vitamin B: yeast extract, whole meal bread, wheat germ, cereals, liver, beef, pork, bacon, cheese, fish, ham, whole-milk, rolled oats.

Vitamin C: fresh citrus fruits, vegetables, tomatoes, fresh strawberries, cantaloupe, cabbage, broccoli, green pepper (capsicum).

Vitamin D: milk, butter, margarine, egg yolk, liver, sardines, tuna, salmon.

The Healthiest Heartwise Foods

These antioxidant-rich foods are nutrient-dense, containing health-promoting phytonutrients. It is important to note that the risk of heart disease is two times greater for women than for men. The following foods are considered fat-releasers:

1. Almonds, cashews, walnuts, pecans, peanuts (Five times weekly).
2. Extra virgin olive oil or olives (Two tablespoons daily).
3. Coffee (one to six cups daily).
4. Alcohol in moderation daily (Five ounces red wine, one ounce liquor, 12 ounces beer).
5. Cinnamon (one teaspoon daily).
6. Green tea (five times daily).
7. Dark chocolate (The darker the chocolate, the higher the polyphenols/antioxidant content. Chocolate contains protein, carbohydrate, iron, potassium, calcium, and may help lower blood pressure and increase HDL (good cholesterol) and does not raise LDL (bad cholesterol); it acts much like an aspirin).
8. Vinegar (Balsamic or apple cider).
9. Tomatoes (calcium magnesium).
10. Wild sockeye salmon, herring, sardines (vitamin B12, omega 3, protein, selenium), catfish, tuna, shrimp, mackerel (rich in omega 3), or any fatty fish (eat fatty fish three times a week).
11, Whole grains (bulgur wheat, brown rice, oatmeal, shredded wheat, popcorn).
12. Free range eggs.
13. Cod liver oil.

14. Sweet potatoes, garlic, onions, spinach, beans, oats, soy, shitake mushrooms, (for vitamins B1 & B2), and broccoli, which along with traditional vitamins and minerals, also contains sulforaphane, indoles, carotenoids, beta-carotene, lutein, and zeathanin that helps prevent macular degeneration, which can lead to blindness in older adults.

15. Berries of all types are credited with fending-off memory loss and the mental decline of aging. Blueberries and strawberries are rich in a type of flavonoid called anthocyanidins, which are known to cross from the blood into the brain and locate in the parts involved in learning and memory. Flavonoids may also help mitigate the effects of stress and inflammation. Gogi (a berry) is considered a cross between a cherry and a cranberry, and is rich in antioxidants. Quinoa contains all eight essential amino-acids.

    Acai, contains Vitamins A & C, and omega fatty acids six and nine.

    Kiwi-fruit is rich in Vitamin C, potassium, and fiber.

    Pomegranate is considered dental floss for your arteries.

    Red skinned grapes, eight ounces daily, help unclog your arteries.

    Cantaloupe melon is antioxidant rich and reduces toxic LDL cholesterol.

    Cranberry juice: drinking eight liquid ounces three times weekly strains and absorbs artery fat.

16. Sunshine is the best source of natural Vitamin D and helps prevent depression.

Definitions:

Phytonutrients: These natural compounds are found in plants. They appear to be potent disease fighters because of their antioxidant properties.

Antioxidants: Think of antioxidants as rust fighters. They protect the body from rust (oxidation) by free radicals. Oxidation is the enemy because it speeds up aging and leads to disease.

Carotenoids: found in red, orange, and yellow pigments in fruits and vegetables, carotenoids include beta-carotene, one of the best-known antioxidants, as well as lutein, lycopene and zeaxanthin.

Polyphenols: A large group of antioxidants, including anthocy-canins, catechins, ellagic acid, quercetin and other substances.

Special Advisory and Disclaimer Note:

• • • • • • • • • • •

Buy a good low-fat cookbook, such as the one published by the American Heart Association, and consult your physician if you have any questions regarding statements in this book.

Heimlich Maneuver

Unfortunately, most countries and U.S. states do not mandate Heimlich Maneuver training for restaurant employees, although I believe at least one employee per shift, be it management, dining room, kitchen, or other staff, should be certified or receive education and training in the technique. Regardless of the cost (if any) to the employer, it should be the law!

The Heimlich Maneuver is a simple but very, very important and effective life saving procedure. It is a technique that is not difficult to learn, and the American Red Cross does offer training on it for a nominal fee.

Trainees should expect to be tested annually for competency.

It is much easier to learn than first aid or cardio pulmonary resusitation (CPR), and the technique has not changed, and is not expected to change or vary, any time soon.

It may be performed on an infant under age one, a baby, a child, an adult, an obese adult, a pregnant female, a dog, and even oneself by leaning over a chair or a table.

I myself suffered a choking episode one evening during dinner. Fortunately, my close friend who was dining with me knew what to do, he performed the Heimlich Maneuver and saved me. Unfortunately, I've known a family medical physician who was not so lucky. While he was dining at a restaurant, a piece of steak stuck in his windpipe. No other patron, or staff member knew what to do, and the good doctor died.

1. When a person is choking, the first action should come from that victim him or herself, by giving the "International Distress

Sign For Choking," which is done by placing both hands across each other on one's throat.

2. It is important to remember that the human brain requires oxygen. When a conscious victim starts to choke, it's because he or she has an obstruction in the windpipe (or airway), and if it is not quickly cleared by forcing air from the lungs up the windpipe (or airway) to expel that obstruction within four to six minutes, the brain starts to die off. After six to10 minutes the brain is dead and damage is permanent and irreversible, and the victim will then die.

3. If the victim is talking or coughing, leave him or her alone. Coughing is good and indicates his or her airway is somewhat clear, and he or she will most likely clear the obstruction themselves.

4. Don't invite conversation with a victim, therefore, do NOT ask a choking victim questions such as, "Are you O.K.?" Remember, he or she cannot verbally respond. Simply tell the victim you are going to perform the Heimlich Maneuver.

5. Stand the victim up straight (the Heimlich can also be performed with the victim laying down on his or her back).

6. Make a fist with your RIGHT hand, place your LEFT hand over your RIGHT fist, and place BOTH fists just above the victim's belly-button, and just below the rib-cage. Then thrust BOTH fists upward towards the victims head in a "J" thrust five times as hard as you can. If unsuccessful in removing the obstruction, check the victim's face to re-assess the coloration of the face, and repeat the process again as hard as you can.

7. If still unsuccessful, call 911 immediately.

8. In the case of a pregnant female, do NOT touch the belly. Instead, place BOTH fists at the chest cleavage area, and thrust up and down.

9. Every restaurant and kitchen should also have a separate first aid kit on hand for emergency situations.

Chef's Knives

Most chefs will agree that the most important working tools to him are his knives. A chef cherishes his knives just like Renoir cherished his brushes, and they are in constant use preparing just about every recipe.

Professional chefs knives have for centuries been designed, forged, tempered, ground, buffed, honed, and triple riveted with old-world craftsmanship by artisans, and with input about ergonomic design by great chefs throughout Europe.

Chefs always wash and wipe their knives dry after every use...a chef's knives are his babies. We protect and care for them as we protect and care for our families. Most chefs should maintain a minimum inventory of knives as follows:

1. 2 ¾-inch Peeling Knife.
2. 3 or 4-inch Paring Knives.
3. 5-inch serrated Utility Knife.
4. 5 ½-inch Boning Knife.
5. 6, or 8, or 10-inch Chefs Kni
6. 10-inch Slicing Knife.
7. 8-inch serrated Bread Knife.
8. Cleaver
9. 10-inch Sharpening Steel.

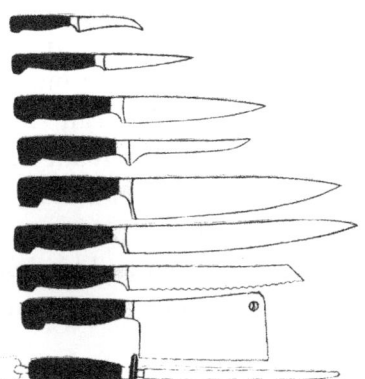

How to use a Sharpening Steel

• • • • • • • • • • •

1. Place the heel of the blade (the cutting edge near the knife handle) towards the tip of the sharpening steel.
2. Hold the knife blade at a 20-degree angle to the steel.
3. Slowly pull the knife DOWN and ACROSS the steel in a slight 45-degree arc. Repeat this motion on the other side of the steel.
4. Repeat these steps five to10 times, always alternating the right and left side of the cutting edge.
5. Using speed is not critical; it is more important to maintain the 20-degree angle of the cutting edge of the knife against the steel in order to sharpen the full length of the blade.

"The King of Chefs and the Chef of Kings"

To the memory of the great Maitre Chef Auguste Escoffier, whose culinary career, superb creativity, and outstanding accomplishments were a masterpiece, and who inspired me to continuously pursue culinary perfection.

AUGUSTE ESCOFFIER
October 28, 1846 - February 12, 1935
"La bonne cuisine est la base du veritable bonheur"
("Good cooking is the source of true happiness")
A. Escoffier

• • • • • • • • • •

I have been an ardent admirer of Monsieur Escoffier my entire culinary career, and I would be remiss if I did not bring his illustrious life-story to your attention.

You should take inspiration from the fact that he was a little boy from a tiny French village who became a giant in the culinary world. Therefore, I believe it is very important that apprentice chefs and novice cooks who read this acquire an appreciation for him, for he was the master of all chefs, and is still to this day the symbol of the high quality of unique, authentic, and extraordinary French cooking that he bestowed upon the world.

He was a diminutive man who wore custom-made platform shoes in order to comfortably reach the stove in his early years. He quickly rose to become regarded as the Emperor of the world's kitchens (an honorary title conferred upon him by Emperor William the Second of Germany), the Ambassador of French Cuisine, and was eventually made a Chevalier of the Legion of Honour in 1920 by French President Raymond Poincare in London, and a rosette of an Officer of the Legion from French Prime Minister Edouard Herriot at a magnificent banquet held in his honor at the Palais d'Orsay in Paris in 1928.

His brilliant professional career began in 1859 at age 13 in his uncle's "Restaurant Francais" in Nice, France, and lasted 62 years until he decided to retire to Monte Carlo in 1921 at age 74, where he died on February 12, 1935 at age 89, a few days after the death of his wife, the poet Delphine Daffis.

They were survived by three children.

Monsieur Escoffier is buried in the family vault in his hometown village of Villeneuve-Loubet, France.

Seldom, if ever, has any chef had such a supreme professional career. It is estimated that his sage advice resulted in training nearly 2,000 apprentice chefs during the artistic course of his culinary life.

He co-created, (along with Cesar Ritz) the Ritz Hotel chain, and authored seven classic cookbooks: *L'Aide-Memoire Culinaire*, *Ma Cuisine*, *Le Livre des Menu's*, *Les Fleurs en Cire*, *Le Riz*, *Le Carnet d'Epicure*, *La Morue*, and co-authored (with Phileas Gilbert and E. Fetu) *Le Guide Culinaire*.

He also created the idea of A La Carte dining and the French brigade system of stations in the professional kitchen, which improved the organization and speed of kitchen operations.

He was known as "Papa" to his colleagues, and it was his staff that perished on the *Titanic*—he had designed the elaborate menus for that ill-fated voyage. Afterwards, he personally provided financial assistance to the families of his staff who were on board the *Titanic*.

He slept only four to five hours daily, and was a non-smoker and non-alcohol user. He also forbade profanity and brutality in his kitchen.

Monsieur Escoffier chose St. Fortunat (born 530) to be the patron Saint of chefs, because he was a culinary poet, and former Arch-Bishop of Poitiers, France.

I recommend that aspiring chefs visit Monsieur Escoffier's birthplace and childhood family home (as I did in September 1993), which has been restored and converted into a culinary museum. It is located in his charming hometown village of Villeneuve-Loubet in the south of France, just minutes north from the Mediterranean, between Nice and Antibes on the Cote-D'Azur.

The address is: Musee de L'art Culinaire, 3 Rue Escoffier, Villeneuve-Loubet, Alpes-Maritimes, France. Telephone: 93 20 80 51 Fax: 93 73 93 79

Contact the museum for the current hours of operation.

The name of the street was changed to Rue Escoffier in 1957 in his honor.

Also, visit his statue and monument erected in 1936 in front of City Hall; I am confident you will come away inspired to do great things.

I am very well aware that he was preceded by other notable French connoisseurs-gastronomes such as Jean Brillat-Savarin, Jean-Jacques Cambaceres, Antonin Careme, Grimod De La Reyniere, and Charles Talleyrand, some of whom were more noted as barristers-at-law, politicians, diplomats, and magistrates and later followed by the famed French restaurateur Fernand Point (1897-1955). Other than Careme and Point, they were not "working chefs," devoting long arduous hours and their entire life to the culinary profession as did the predominant Monsieur Escoffier. It is for this laborious reason his legend will never be equaled.

Monsieur Escoffier's family birthplace and home in Villaneuve-Loubet, France, now a Culinary Art Museum.

Employment

A good chef does not really "find" a new job.

He/she identifies, evaluates, and seizes the opportunity to better him/her self.

Before accepting any verbal or written offer of employment for a culinary position from an establishment, a chef should request a written employment proposal stating the following:

1. The position offered, its responsibilities, its benefit's, and its privileges (such as complimentary use of a golf course with cart, tennis courts, swimming pool, spa, gym, etcetera).
2. A commencement date, an annual base salary, bonuses, details of salary payment, maximum and minimum hours and days per week, paid annual vacation, paid holidays, paid floating holidays, paid sick, and paid family bereavement day entitlements.
3. Eligibility for benefits should include major medical health, dental, long-term disability, and accidental death and dismemberment insurance.
4. A 180-day performance evaluation period, and if satisfactory, a resultant salary increase.
5. A clause identifying your immediate supervisor or director.
6. The prospective employee should expect to undergo a drug screen and background check, with random drug and alcohol screens from time to time during the course of employment. A failure of these tests usually results in disciplinary action up to, and including termination of employment.
7. A 90-day probationary period is normal. This probationary period

gives both the employer and the employee the opportunity to asses each other. Termination options usually hold equally for both parties during this period.

8. Additionally a 401-K plan is most times available after 90 days of employment. Company contributions to this plan are usually at the sole discretion of the company.

9. A company employee handbook detailing company core values and personnel policies and procedures should always be issued to each new employee.

10. In most cases, an employee will be required to sign a confidentiality agreement in order to protect the proprietary information and trade secrets of the company.

When preparing a written resume, do NOT lie! It will come back to haunt you. Most importantly, before accepting any culinary position, the FIRST priority a chef must satisfy him/her self with is the cleanliness of the establishment. If it does not meet his/her cleanliness expectations....WALK AWAY!

Restaurant executives should realize that running a spotlessly sanitized, clean restaurant is a no-brainer. Aside from the restaurant's customer base, the employee's word of mouth recommendation with his/her families, friends, and wide circle-of-influence can result in boosting a tremendous ongoing amount of business.

I believe one of the most important things an employer can do to retain good, young culinary employees is to provide them with proper training and development.

I believe properly training an employee is an investment...not an expense.

I believe in coaching employees rather than managing them.

I believe happier, motivated employees result in efficient service, and ensure lasting relationships with one's customers.

I believe if one thinks training an employee, and watching them leave you is expensive, imagine not training them and watching them stay.

Great employees are the foundation of any company, and knowing that employees can either make or break a company, I believe proprietors and companies would be wise to offer a financial profit sharing "reward for productivity" program for employees. In today's business environment, companies reward their executives with millions of dollars in bonuses, why not the average employee?

I once worked at a London establishment whereby the directors paid every employee one penny per customer served at the end of each week. It was a tremendous incentive over and above our salaries. The weekly bonus was always a respectable amount, and it definitely encouraged us to go that extra mile.

An English penny certainly seems insignificant today, however in 1964 it was worth a lot more than it is today, and when added up usually represented between ten and twenty percent of our gross weekly salaries depending on how busy we were.

It was certainly an appreciated gratuity.

Culinary employees should be passionate and take great pride in preparing and serving fresh, high quality food and beverages to their guests in order to create a memorable dining experience each time.

If not...get out of the business!

Always remember the motto.....

"We are ladies and gentlemen, serving ladies and gentlemen."

Culinary Consulting

One of the best lessons I ever learned while consulting is that you must first figure out what policies and procedures the organization had been practicing that brought them to the point of needing the services of a consultant, and then determine if they have the heart, and the willingness to consider capital expenditure to do what it will take to improve their position.

During previous culinary consultations, I have experienced deplorable and disgusting kitchen and bathroom conditions, and as a result of my emphasis about hygiene, and my scathing written report of other violations, I have been responsible for the closure of several restaurants for refurbishment.

The first place I inspect when consulting is not the kitchen or dining room, but the bathrooms. There is no doubt whatsoever that the bathrooms are where killer bacteria and disease flourish and thrive.

If a restaurant has dirty bathrooms, customers are immediately turned off and will not continue patronizing the establishment.

Most times I find that I need to recommend a complete bathroom renovation.

The following is a sample "Culinary Consultation Contract."

This contract was written and used by the author without obtaining legal advice, and is presented here as simply a guide to work from.

The reader is advised to seek advice from his/her own legal counsel before copying, reproducing, or entering into this contract.

Chef Patrick J. Gorey

Culinary Consultation Contract

• • • • • • • • • •

Consultant Name: Independent Professional Chef

Address: Culinary Consultant

Phone: E-Mail:

• • • • • • • • • •

(In this section, state your education, training and employment history)

• • • • • • • • • •

This contract is specifically preconditioned and contingent upon the following terms and conditions, and in consideration of the mutual covenants contained herein, and the compensation and services hereinafter mentioned and provided, the parties hereby agree as follows:

This contract entered into this _____ day of _____ ,

_____ by and between Chef

- _____ (Hereinafter referred to

as "CONSULTANT:") and _____

_____

_____

(Hereinafter referred to as "CUSTOMER"), whose business address is:

_____

_____

Whereas, Consultant is in the business of providing culinary advice & recommendations. Whereas, Customer wishes to obtain such services.

1. SERVICE PROVIDED BY CONSULTANT

Consultant shall enter upon Customer's place of business for the sole and only purpose of inspecting, reviewing, and evaluating the Customer's place of business and its employees, and the function and operation, in order to arrive at a professional opinion, to include the following:

Food Purchasing, Personnel Management, Analyzing and Maintaining Excellent Food Costs, Inventory Evaluation, Menu Customization, Employee Time and Motion, Employee Attitude, Respect, Motivation and Satisfaction, Dining Room Overview, Cleanliness Review, Theft and Waste Elimination.

2. OBLIGATIONS OF CONTRACT

Consultant shall conduct an inspection, review, and evaluation within ___ calendar days of the aforesaid date of this contract, and shall be on site for a MAXIMUM time period of 10 business hours. Consultant shall provide Customer with a written report covering the items stated in paragraph 1 of this contract, within 30 business days of the execution of this contract as stated below.

3. COMPENSATION

Customer shall pay to Consultant the sum of.......................... Dollars per hour, for 10 hours, for a total of............................... Dollars, which shall be paid to Consultant within three business days of Customer's receipt of a written report of the aforesaid review and inspection from Consultant. In the event said payment is not received by Consultant within the aforesaid specified time, Consultant shall immediately proceed with filing a court action against Customer in order to recover said payment, plus ALL costs, legal and otherwise, as incurred by such inaction.

4. CONFIDENTIALITY CLAUSE

Consultant and Customer shall maintain strict and complete confidentiality regarding this inspection, review, evaluation and subsequent written report.

5. RELEASE

Customer hereby releases, quit claims and forever discharges Consultant, his Employees and any Officer, Partner or Spouse of any one of them, and any other Person, Firm or Corporation who may be liable by or through them, from any and all claims, losses or demands, including but not limited to any consequence, whether now known or not, which may arise from this inspection, review, evaluation, and written report.

THIS RELEASE SHALL SURVIVE THIS CONTRACT.

6. ENTIRE CONTRACT

This contract shall be binding on Customer's heirs, successors, assigns or nominees. Customer hereby acknowledges that a full, complete copy of this contract was furnished for examination and approval prior to execution thereof.

All other terms and conditions of this contract shall remain unchanged and in full force and effect.

IN WITNESS WHEREOF the parties have hereunto set their hands and seals the day, month and years as stated below.

CUSTOMER: _____   WITNESS _____

DATE _____

CUSTOMER_____   WITNESS _____

DATE _____

CONSULTANT_____   WITNESS _____

DATE _____

Buffet Artistry

Some examples of Buffet Artistry from the author's collection.

French Charolais Bull Ice Carving

Grandmother in Rocking Chair Ice Carving

Swan Ice Carving

Pretzel Pastilliage Nativity Scene

Pretzel Log Cabin

Bread Basket

Pastilliage Clubhouse Model by the Author Circa 1970

Gingerbread Village Scene

Napkin Folding

Fleur-de-lis / Bishops Hat

Fold napkin into a triangle. Fold right and left corners down to the bottom point. Fold down top point of diamond to within one inch of the bottom. Then fold this point back up to top edge. Turn over and fold the left and right sides towards the center, and tuck one side into the fold of the other. For "fleur-de-lis," fold down the flaps on each side of the hat. For a different look, tuck the flaps into the cuff.

Bird of Paradise/Sailboat

Fold napkin in half and then fold again into a quarter. Fold again into a triangle. Make sure to keep loose edges on inside of triangle. Fold the two sides down from point of triangle where the loose edges are. Fold the two points at bottom edge under. Then fold in half (so the two points that were just folded underneath are on the inside facing each other) and pull up edges to form the flower or sails.

Swan

Cut a piece of aluminum foil a bit smaller than the napkin and place on top of the napkin. From one corner start rolling up napkin to form a long tube. Shape the napkin to form a swan. (You can put a small piece of tape under to hold tube in place.) Then place the Bird-of-Paradise over the top of the swan shape to form feathers of the swan. This can be used as a center-piece. This shape looks good with white, starched damask napkins.

Single Candle

Fold napkin into triangle with the point at the bottom and fold down from the top approximately one to two inches to create a cuff. Turn over and fold up the bottom point no further than the top edge. Choose one of the corners and fold straight down where the bottom point used to be (creates flame, should be sticking out at the bottom). Then roll up napkin lengthwise starting at the folded side and finish by tucking the other corner into cuff. Stand the candle on the table. This shape can be done in alternative colors of red or green for Christmas or any color to suit the theme.

Pleated Fan

Fold napkin in half to make a rectangle. Then pleat napkin into one-inch accordion pleats leaving the last six inches unfolded. Fold in half with pleats on the outside. Fold down the top corner and tuck into pleats. Stand napkin on table to form a fan.

Double Candle

Fold napkin into a triangle. Fold corners on both left and right sides about three inches in. Then fold the points out again to create two flames on either side. Start rolling the napkin lengthwise starting at the long edge towards the bottom point. Fold the rolled napkin in half and place in glass.

Tuxedo Shirt

Fold napkin into triangle shape with the point at the bottom. Fold down a cuff at the top and flip the napkin over. Then take each corner on the left and right and fold down about two inches past the bottom point, forming the jacket. Tuck under both corners at the bottom and also tuck away a little bit of material on each side for clean edges all over. If possible, place a small bow-tie to finish napkin. This can be used to indicate the gentlemen's places at the table and perhaps use the pleated fan for ladies.

Elf Boot

Open napkin and fold left and right sides to the center. Then fold napkin down from top about 2/3 down and flip around. Fold down both top corners to meet in the middle to look like a house. Then fold top edges down again to meet along the center so it looks like an airplane. Then fold in half lengthwise. Hold the smooth surface up and point facing to one side. Take one part of the "tail" and turn up alongside seam. Take the other "tail," wrap around back of the first one and tuck off the point. Turn down the first "tail" to form a cuff or sock.

Water Lily
Place napkin open and fold in corners to center (four times). Repeat this move two more times. Turn over napkin and again repeat move (corners into center). Then, very carefully start to pull out edges from under napkin at each corner. Only pull out first corners, then second and third folds from underneath. The final effect should be a flower shape, which can be used as a table center to hold flowers etc., or wine glass can be stood in center.

Buffet Fold
Fold napkin into quarter. Make sure open edges are on top right side. Fold down first edge from top right-hand side to bottom left-hand side. Then fold down second edge and tuck into top of first fold. Fold the two sides under so that they cross over at the back. Place cutlery into pocket. Can be used very effectively with different colored napkins in paper or used as a napkin for a place setting, using the pocket for a place card, a flower or a greeting card, etc.

Entertaining with Ease

Guidelines for a successful fine dining experience.

1. Hosts should be completely hands free and happy to meet and greet their guests.

2. Remember to see that guests are well cared for. This is about them, not just you. From the first to the last guest, maintain a spirit of relaxed gaiety and atmosphere.

3. Pre-set the dinner table and bar the day before. Make extra space in the refrigerator, (minimum two shelves), and make sure the oven is clean.

4. Inquire if any guest has a food allergy, intolerance, dietary requirement, or vegetarian concern. Keep a logbook on your friends' specific preferences for future reference.

5. Have perfectly mixed drinks, tempered wines of the guests' tastes, cooled (not chilled) plain champagne (if serving), cooled beer and sodas, linen cocktail napkins if possible (if not, use paper), coffee and tea-making capabilities.

6. Purchase plenty of ice cubes (never run out!).

7. Have corkscrew, bottle opener, ice tongs, fresh lemons, and water glasses for dinner table. Arrange for a prepared bartender who knows that his or her place is behind the bar.

8. Hors d'oeuvre (if serving) may be placed on a side table, or passed on trays. They should be tasty, piquant tidbits, olives, crisp celery or fennel, etc, (no cheese) in order to stimulate the appetite, not dull it.

9. Use best china, linen dinner napkins (no paper), silverware, crystal or clear glassware, candles and candleholders, cruets, fresh flowers or greenery (low in center of table), subdued overhead lighting, breadbaskets, and votives if using.

10. Serve gourmet, tasty food of the highest quality with efficient service (Chef recommends no breads if serving potatoes, and vice versa).

11. The Chef should create, provide, and sign individually typed menus with each guest's name, which can then be used in the place setting.

Ten Tips for a Cleaner Safer Kitchen

1. Refrigerator

    Wipe handles daily. Discard past-date foods. Wipe up spills promptly. Every three months, empty and clean shelves with ¼ cup baking soda to one quart warm water, then spray with a 50% white vinegar/water solution and air dry. Clean rubber gasket inside door to ensure a tight seal.

    NEVER thaw frozen meats/poultry or seafood on kitchen counter.

    Do so in refrigerator while covered. Keep raw and cooked foods separately, and sealed in airtight containers.

    If you suffer a long, protracted power outage, dump everything!

    Use leftovers within three to four days so mold doesn't have a chance to grow. Placing an opened box of baking soda (sodium bicarbonate-Na $HCo3$) in the refrigerator will NOT attract, or absorb odors. This does absorb and neutralize bacterial spores and acid molecules, (Butyric, Caproic, Caprylic) from fat. Activated charcoal is best, but let's face it: prevention is the ONLY antidote!

2. Counters

    Clean regularly with an all-purpose cleaner, then spray with a 50% white vinegar-water solution, or spray with a weak bleach-water solution and air dry.

3. Cutting Boards

    Solid wood cutting boards without separation seams are safest as long as they are kept clean, sanitized, and dry.

    Studies show that wood hampers bacteria growth, while bacteria thrives in crevices on plastic boards. If overly scarred with crevices...

throw them out. Sanitize wooden boards by spritzing them with a weak bleach/water, soapy water, or a white vinegar/water solution after each use.

Chefs / Cooks should retain four wooden cutting boards and identify one each for PRODUCE, MEATS, POULTRY, and FISH.

Remember to wash and clean knives IMMEDIATELY after use. Always cover cuts with bandages.

4. Dish Towels/Sponges
Change dish towels and sponges DAILY.

5. Dishes and Dishwashers
If dishes are hand washed and rinsed, air-dry in a rack.
To reduce soap build-up in a dishwasher, occasionally fill the soap dispenser with baking soda, or place a small cup of white vinegar on the top shelf and run the dishwasher until empty.

6. Sink, Dish Drainer, Faucet Handles, and Trash Can Lids.
Clean regularly with household cleanser.

7. Stove, Oven, and Hood.
Oven spills are not a food hazard if you regularly heat the oven to 400 degrees F. Hood extractor vents should be removed, washed with a soapy/water solution, and air dried.

8. Microwave
Fill a bowl with two cups water and one whole lemon cut into slices.
Microwave for two minutes, then wipe out with paper towels and discard.

9. Pet Bowls
Do NOT clean turtle, frog, goldfish, or pet bowls in the kitchen sink. Use a separate bucket and discard in the toilet.

10. Cross-contamination
   • Do NOT put COOKED food on the same surface you used for RAW food.
   • Pay attention and sanitize what you have touched after handling raw foods.

- Use alcohol-based sanitizer.
- Thoroughly wash (as many as three times) and peel raw fruits and vegetables.
- Fast-food or residential playland areas for children need to be thoroughly disinfected and sanitized every DAY!
- Immediately wash toilet tank handle after use.

A Typical Sample Culinary Quiz Given at High-Level Chef Employment Interviews

Created by the author
(Answers below)

1. How many liquid tablespoons in a cup?
2. How many liquid cups are in a gallon?
3. How many ounces are in a pound?
4. Define the word hors d'oeuvre.
5. What are hors d'oeuvre?
6. What is the difference between an hors d'oeuvre and a canapé?
7. What is stock?
8. What is broth?
9. What is bouillon?
10. What is consommé?
11. Define clarification of bouillon / stock for consommé.
12. What is demi-glace?
13. What is jus lie?
14. What is a bouquet garni?
15. What is a roux, and what is it used for?
16. What is a slurry (culinary), and what is it used for?
17. What is buerre manie, and what is it used for?
18. Name the five basic or "mother" sauces.
19. Name the three most famous chilled soups.
20. What is bouillabaisse?
21. Define the words sauté, fry, broil.

22. Name at least 10 types of lettuce or salad greens.
23. Name the three main ingredients in salad dressing.
24. Name at least six uncommon cheeses.
25. Name five common large cuts of beef.
26. Name at least 10 types of saltwater fish.
27. Name the four basic presses for olive oil.
28. At what temperature should eggs be kept stored?
29. What does baking soda consist of?
30. What are the three ingredients in baking powder?

Answers

· · · · · · · · · · ·

1. 16 = 48 teaspoons = 8 ozs.
2. 16.
3. 16.
4. Hors d'oeuvre means "Outside the meal," or "outside the work."
5. Appetizing tidbits prior to a meal.
6. An hors d'oeuvre is a small, tasty tidbit, hot or cold, in a sauce or marinade. A canapé is either toast, biscuit, or pastry shell, topped with savory butters, pastes, or small tidbits.
7. The liquid from the process of boiling roasted meat bones & vegetables.
8. The un-clarified liquid from the process of boiling meat pieces & vegetables.
9. Reduced brown stock.
10. Beef stock, which has been enriched, concentrated and clarified.
11. Whip the whites & shells of two eggs (for a small volume) lightly with the lukewarm bouillon/stock, and the green of leeks, celery, and parsley stalks. Continue to stir with a wooden spoon over heat until boiling is established. Move the pot to the side of the heat and simmer (not boil) for 30 minutes, approximately. Finally, strain the consommé TWICE through a fine muslin cloth.
12. The reduction, for approximately three hours, of half espagnole sauce (Brown Sauce), and half basic, clear veal and/or beef stock until it is reduced by half and takes on a brilliant, thick glaze. Finish the sauce with Madeira or dry sherry.

13. The reduction of roasted veal bones and vegetable stock thickened with a "slurry" of arrowroot-starch and water, or cornstarch and water. Flavor the sauce with dry marsala wine and serve. Mainly used for veal dishes.

14. Fresh herbs, peppercorns and bay leaves tied in a bundle of cheesecloth and added to stock.

15. Melted, clarified butter and plain flour slowly cooked over low heat until the desired color is attained. There are three roux stages; WHITE (for bechamel & veloutes), BLOND (for tomato soup and other mid-colored cooked mixtures), and BROWN (for espagnole sauce and other dark mixtures). Brown roux is usually baked in a copper pot in the oven while stirring it with a wooden spoon frequently until the desired color is attained. The color of each stage is determined by the amount of time the blend is cooked. Roux is then used as a thickening base for sauces and soups. Buerre Manie, or slurry, does almost the same thing.

16. A fluid mixture of either flour and water or cornstarch (or arrowroot-starch) and water.

    A culinary slurry is then used as a thickening agent for soups, sauces, stews, and casseroles (The word "slurry" is also used when mixing cement and water).

17. A compound of five tablespoons (75 grams) of butter, and three-quarters cup (100grams) of plain flour, blended into a smooth paste. It is then used as a quick liaison to bind certain soups and sauces.

18. Bechamel, espagnole, tomato, veloute, jus lie.

19. Vichyssoise, consommé Madrilène, Gazpacho.

20. A famous seafood / shellfish dish originating in Marseilles, France.

21. Sautee: To cook in a skillet over a strong heat in butter or oil. Fry: To immerse certain foods in a large, deep pan of hot oil. Broil: To cook on or under a gas gridiron, or under an electric element.

22. Bibb, escarole, curly endive, romaine, red leaf, spinach, French or Belgian endive, Chinese cabbage, iceberg, watercress, frisee, dandelion, fennel.

23. Oil, vinegar, herbs.

24. Stilton, brie, camembert, gouda, port salut, edam, gruyere, gorgonzola, Roquefort.

25. Steamship (hindquarter), baron (sirloin strip), tenderloin, rib roast, top round.

26. Dover sole, plaice, mahi mahi, flounder, cod, halibut, swordfish, herring, brill, turbot, skate.
27. Extra virgin, virgin, classico or lampante, pomace or extra light.
28. Forty degrees Fahrenheit (4.4 degrees Celsius) or below.
29. Bicarbonate of soda (sodium bicarbonate)
30. Cream of tartar, soda (monocalcium phosphate, sodium bicarbonate), cornstarch.

Important Chemical Definitions
Connected to Food

AGAR AGAR: East Indian sea plant with approximately eight times the jellifying power of gelatin.

ALEURON: Vegetable protein substance in wheat. It is used in diabetic diets.

ALKALI: A soda or potash that neutralizes acids and forms salts.

ANTIBIOTIC: Fights bacteria. Is inimical to life.

ANTIBODY: Blood substance to counteract toxins.

ANTISEPTIC: Free of germs.

BENZOIC ACID: A crystallized acid used as an antiseptic preservative.

BORAX: A crystallized salt used in fruit preservation.

CASEIN: Albuminoid / Protein in milk. Also found in vegetables called Legumin.

144

CHLORIDE: A compound of Chlorine with another element.

CHLORINE: A yellow-green poisonous, gaseous element obtained from common salt, used as a disinfectant, and also for bleaching.

CREAM OF TARTAR: Crystallized tartar used in baking powder. Also used instead of glucose in boiling of sugar to prevent formation of sugar crystals.

DEXTRIN: Carbohydrate occurring in decomposition of starch, used as a polisher when dissolved in hot water.

ENZYME: An organic substance that aids in certain transformations of materials in the digestion of food.

GUM ARABIC: Obtained from different species of Acacia. Soluble in water. Used as a glaze.

NITRATES: A salt of nitric acid (colorless, corrosive liquid, aqua-fortis). * Nitric and hydrocloric acids will dissolve gold and platinum.

PLASTICINE: A modelling clay. Plasticine models are used for making plaster or sulfur molds.

SACCHARIN: A substance distilled from coal tar, of great sweetness.

SHELLAC: A chemical glaze used for inedible showpieces.

STERILIZE: To free from bacteria. In fruit preservation, to bring to the boiling point.

SULPHUR: A non-metallic, yellow, brittle element. Used for making molds, whereby the chemical is melted and becomes a liquid substance.

TALCUM: A powder derived from the soapstone. Used to prevent hand perspiration in sugar work, or in candy manufacturing.

TRAGACANTH: Gum provided by several species of plants. Tragacanth gum is used by perfume-makers, confectioners, and pastry chefs to bind their oils or to give body to their pastes.

TARTARIC ACID: Acid found in a large number of fruits and which is extracted from the lees of wine.

WAX: Bee and vegetable wax has a high degree of heat resistance, and is an excellent insulator.

CPSIA information can be obtained at www.ICGtesting.com
Printed in the USA
BVOW11*0416130115

383067BV00002B/2/P